# ROADS LESS TRAVELED

# ROADS LESS TRAVELED

and Other Perspectives on
Nationally Competitive Scholarships

## THE NATIONAL ASSOCIATION OF
## FELLOWSHIPS ADVISORS

———————

*Edited by Suzanne McCray and Joanne Brzinski*

THE UNIVERSITY OF ARKANSAS PRESS
FAYETTEVILLE
2017

ISBN: 978-1-68226-046-3
eISBN: 978-1-61075-623-5

21  20  19  18  17    5  4  3  2  1

Cover design: Morgan Bibbs

∞ The paper used in this publication meets the minimum requirements of the American
National Standard for Permanence of Paper for Printed Library Materials Z39.48–1984.

*Library of Congress Control Number: 2017941834*

# Contents

# Foreword

In July 2015, the National Association of Fellowships Advisors (NAFA) gathered for our eighth biennial conference, "The Road Less Traveled," a meeting designed to encourage members to think past the norms of fellowships advising. From expanding the range of awards institutions support, to recruiting underrepresented candidates for fellowship programs, to thinking beyond the traditional institutions and countries students seek to experience, advisors were challenged to explore creative ways to elevate their approaches to fellowships advising. The conference set a record for attendance, involving 426 members and foundation representatives.

The conference theme was central to the vision for the event. Billed as a San Francisco Bay Area conference, even the location in downtown Oakland (instead of San Francisco) was a less traveled road; this accommodated the limited budgets of higher education, nonprofit, and government members. Conference organizers worked energetically to bring in foundations that had not attended NAFA events before, as well as some that had been absent for some time. Representatives from the Ford, Pickering, Humanity in Action, Public Policy and International Affairs Program, and Hertz were present. The preconference workshop for veteran advisors went down a new path as well, focusing on strategic assessment, a topic often broached by advisors seeking to analyze and measure the effectiveness of their work. In Oakland, after a six-year absence from the conference, a lunch fair promoted summer and other post-baccalaureate activities, equipping advisors with alternative opportunities for students who are not selected for major award programs. There are even changes in the advising roles of conference participants; for several years, the number of members who serve as secondary advisors in established fellowships advising offices has continued to rise. This new breadth in the National Association of Fellowships Advisors is exciting and requires targeted programming for various levels of expertise to best serve this changing membership base.

The keynote speaker was B. Cole, a former Truman, Rotary, and Echoing Green Scholar, who shared her experience applying for fellowships as a student of color and the first in her family to attend college. Cole has dedicated her life to empowering young people through her organization Brioxy, which helps students of color find fellowship and internship opportunities. Cole's message was inspiring and a fitting endnote, galvanizing advisors to return to their campuses with strategies to better serve all student populations.

Since the conference, NAFA has continued to move down roads less traveled as an organization. In 2015, as membership numbers continued their upward trend, the formerly all-volunteer organization hired its first employee. We were fortunate to have a longtime advisor filling this role: John Richardson is one of the organization's founding members and served as treasurer for the first twelve years. In addition, in 2016 a delegation of affiliated advisors pioneered the first study tour outside of Western Europe, spending ten days in Taiwan. This pilot program paved the way for future international ventures currently being explored for 2018.

The organization continues to grow and evolve, necessitating new paths in long-term planning, including rethinking conference planning. The usual schedule of planning major conferences eighteen months in advance is no longer feasible, as a limited number of hotels and conference spaces can accommodate the increasing size of NAFA. For the first time, the logistics for two biennial conferences are being organized concurrently, including the 2017 conference in Philadelphia and plans for the 2019 conference in Minneapolis.

As NAFA matures as an organization, it is important to remain true to its mission and strengths, while strategically anticipating its needs and developing a vision for the future. Just as NAFA founders charted new territory in the organization's infancy, current leaders are working to address change in the foundation and advising landscape and to have NAFA become an even more visible, respected professional organization within the higher education landscape.

No matter what these new directions, NAFA remains focused on the central mission of promoting the full potential of fellowship candidates through the application process and fostering the growth and professionalization of fellowships advising. Supporting advisors with opportunities to learn directly from foundations and each other while fostering a tight-knit community of collaboration has become a significant hallmark of NAFA. Our members are the lifeblood of this organization, and I am continually proud to be a part of this inclusive and welcoming network of colleagues.

This book is in some ways an extension of that network and speaks to the high quality of work advisors and foundations are engaged in across the globe. The insightful chapters from the Goldwater, Madison, and Truman Foundations will prove to be extremely helpful to advisors who assist students navigating the complexities of the scholarship process. Experienced advisors also share best practices, explore key issues, and develop strategies for defining and assessing success; *Roads Less Traveled* will be an essential resource for anyone assisting students.

Dana Kuchem
The Ohio State University
NAFA President, 2015–2017

# Acknowledgments

The National Association of Fellowships Advisors (NAFA) held its eighth biennial conference in July 2015 in Oakland, California. That conference directly resulted in many of the essays included in this volume. Many people contributed to the conference's success. Joanne Brzinski (Emory University) was the president of NAFA at the time of the conference and provided tireless leadership for the two years that preceded it. Dana Kuchem (The Ohio State University) served as vice president prior to the conference and assumed the role of president at the conference's end. One of the main roles of the vice president is to organize this national event, coordinating speakers, calling for papers, organizing sessions, negotiating logistics, and a long list of other responsibilities that come with orchestrating a major event.

Special thanks go to the conference planning committee: Lyn Fulton-John (Vanderbilt University), Laura Damuth (University of Nebraska, Lincoln), Cindy Schaarschmidt (University of Washington, Tacoma), Dana Dudley (Pepperdine University), Keisha John (Florida State University), and Sarah Cox (Florida State University). Alicia Hayes (University of California, Berkeley) was an invaluable partner as chair of the local committee, which also included Olivia Brewer, Laura Cotten (University of Dayton), Dana Dudley (Pepperdine University), Stefanie Ebeling (University of California, Berkeley), Martha Enciso (San Diego State University), Pamela Gwaltney (University of Southern Illinois), Michelle Lopez (San Diego State University), Diane Murk (Stanford University), and Scott Palmer (University of California, Davis). Cindy Schaarschmidt took on the new challenge of planning the Assessment Workshop, and Tony Cashman (College of the Holy Cross) led the planning of the New Advisors Workshop. Riley Cruttenden, conference assistant, kept planning on track. John Richardson continues to be an invaluable asset for NAFA, working first as treasurer (2001–2013), and then as NAFA's first employee (2014–present).

Other board members who contributed to the effort who have not been named elsewhere, but who deserve recognition include David Schug (University of Illinois at Urbana-Champaign), Belinda Redden (University of Rochester), Jill Deans (University of Connecticut), Robin Chang (University of Washington), Stephanie Wallach (Carnegie Mellon University), Mona Pitre-Collins (University of Washington), Lisa Kooperman (Vassar College), and Robyn Curtis (University of Southern Mississippi). Thanks also go to NAFA officers and board members elected since the conference: Kyle Mox, vice president (Arizona State University), Jeff Wing, treasurer (Virginia Commonwealth University), and Brian Souders, secretary (University of Maryland, Baltimore County).

Foundation board members play a key role in NAFA, sharing their expertise with advisors at conferences, during campus visits, and in the proceedings. Special thanks to NAFA Foundation board members Tara Yglesias (Truman Scholarship Foundation) and Sue Sharp (IIE and Boren Fellowships) and to all the foundation members who participated in the structured foundation interviews or "chat" sessions. Representatives who gave generously of their time include Sue Sharp (Boren), Christine O'Brien (Ford), Daniel Kramer (Fulbright), James Smith (Gates Cambridge), Shawna Hurley (Gilman), Frank Gilmore (Goldwater), Kathy Young (Hertz), Mary Denyer (Marshall), Serena Wilson (Mitchell), Joerg Schlatterer (NSF GRFP), Beverly Sanford (Pickering/Woodrow Wilson), Elliot Gerson (Rhodes), Steven Sundstrom (Rotary), Rob Garris (Schwarzman), Tara Yglesias (Truman), and Paula Randler (Udall).

The NAFA publications committee also deserves thanks for its support of this project, especially Lauren Tuckley (NAFA communications director, Georgetown University) and Jennifer Gerz-Escandón (Georgia State University) who not only contributed essays to this collection, but who also administered the 2017 Survey of the Profession. Thanks also go to Monique Bourque, cochair of the publications and technology committee, and members Valeria Hymas (Baruch College), Grant Eustice (St. Olaf College), Suzanne McCray (University of Arkansas), Emily Saras (Florida State University), Kelly Thornburg (University of Iowa), and John Richardson (University of Louisville). Jesse Delaney (University of Arkansas) richly deserves recognition as well for his work on the survey.

Thanks go to faculty and staff members at Emory University including Michael Elliott (interim dean of the Emory College of Arts and Sciences) and his predecessor, Robin Forman (now vice president at Tulane University), for supporting this work. Andrea Lentz (assistant director of programs) in Emory's Office for Undergraduate Education also deserves thanks. Thanks go as well to the Office of Enrollment Services at the University of Arkansas with special thanks to the staff of the Office of Nationally Competitive Awards in particular. Jonathan Langley (assistant director), Emily Voight (assistant director), and Josh Idaszak (graduate assistant) provided excellent proofreading support. Morgan Bibbs (director of communications in the J. William Fulbright College of Arts and Sciences) designed the striking cover. The continuing support of Dean Michael Miller in the College of Education and Health Professions and Ketevan Mamiseishvili (department chair of Rehabilitation, Human Resources and Communication Disorders) has been greatly appreciated. Thanks as well to University of Arkansas chancellor Joseph Steinmetz and provost Jim Coleman for their support of the Office of Nationally Competitive Awards. This publication would not be possible without the excellent work of the University of Arkansas Press: Mike Bieker (director), David Scott Cunningham (senior editor), and Melissa King (marketing director).

# ROADS LESS TRAVELED

# Introduction

Universities and colleges across the country continue to expand their support for students applying for national and international scholarships. That the National Association of Fellowships Advisors (NAFA) has grown to almost 1,000 individual members is a reflection of this increased focus. Awards remain limited, however, even with the addition of scholarships like the Schwarzman, and so universities have an ever increasing interest in making sure their students have access to accurate information, receive appropriate encouragement, and benefit from informed support during the various stages of what can be an intense process. These collective efforts have enlarged the number of students in the pool, creating scholarship opportunities for students who might not have previously applied, but also necessarily increasing the worthy many who are denied an award.

In order to broaden opportunities for students, many fellowships advising offices are also reaching beyond simply recruiting students for and advising them on scholarship and fellowship applications. Many advisors now support student engagement in other forms, encouraging participation in study abroad and undergraduate research earlier in the student's career, and assisting with a greater range of internship and co-op options. Scholarship offices often address issues associated with need-based aid and the lack of diversity on campus and/or in the application pool. More advisors are also partnering with their campus's study abroad offices, financial aid offices, volunteer action centers, undergraduate research offices, and career centers to help students focus on larger overall career goals and not become overly invested in a particular application.

The title of this volume reflects this expanding purview. Advisors are pursuing roads less traveled for themselves and for their offices, and in many cases are encouraging their students to do the same. The essays included here developed, for the most part, out of presentations and conversations that occurred at NAFA's eighth record-setting biennial conference,

"The Road Less Traveled," held in Oakland, California, in 2015. The volume is divided into four parts—the first provides assessments from three foundations (Truman, Goldwater, and Madison), the second focuses on different avenues for serving students effectively, the third addresses issues about access at student and program levels, and the fourth examines the development of the profession and its place in higher education.

Andy Rich in "Public Service, Power, and the Challenges Facing Millennials," the volume's first essay, calls on the fellowships advising community to engage students in "questions of power, politics, service, and democracy" in order to encourage them to consider public service generally and governmental service specifically as a way of making real differences in their communities and as a means to "fixing things" at state, national, and global levels. His essay is a compelling analysis of why millennials are turning away from government work and toward social entrepreneurship; it also offers hope that this tide can be shifted and that advisors can participate in making that happen.

John Mateja, the new president of the Barry Goldwater Scholarship and Excellence in Education Foundation, provides a brief history of the Goldwater program and a report on recent changes to it in chapter 2. Even more helpfully, he includes an analysis of two recent surveys: one of almost 7,000 former or current scholars about their experiences with the scholarship and one of Goldwater advisors about campus impact. What may be most telling for advisors is the way in which some are using success with the Goldwater program to bring about change for both student and faculty cultures on their campuses. Advisors report that more students are engaging in undergraduate research on their campuses and that more faculty are also increasingly finding room for undergraduates in their labs. Some first-year experience programs are also starting to include undergraduate research as a requirement for its students. Even students who are not nominated by their campuses indicate that the act of applying is an enriching experience, helping them develop a concrete career plan. A vibrant nomination process can result in increases in both faculty mentoring and student engagement on many campuses even as the actual scholarship opportunities remain the same.

Chapter 3 focuses on the James Madison Scholarship. Claire Griffin, the director of special projects for the fellowship foundation, provides a brief history of the program and its requirements and then has previous fellows explain in their own voices the importance of the program's mission: educating high school students on the Constitution. They also outline strategies for advisors who hope to recruit students for the scholarship and for students on the application process.

The final foundation essay comes from Tara Yglesias in chapter 4. Her essay's title "Suspenders and a Belt: Overpreparation and the Overachiever" provides a glimpse of what is to come—an essay that is both fun to read and essential for advisors to understand. This is not Yglesias's first contribution to a NAFA volume. She has written several over the years ("Non Ducor, Duco: Leadership and the Truman Scholarship Application," "Enough about Me, What Do You Think About Me? Surviving the Truman Interview," "I Love It When a Grad Plan Comes Together: Graduate School Advising and the Truman Application"), and each piece has become an important advising tool, frequently shared with students. "Suspenders and a Belt" examines why students come to interviews "overscripted, overwrought, and overprepared." Yglesias suggests advisors may want to tone down their efforts so that an "authentic" person from the institution can have a real conversation with panelists, and in the end, have a much better chance at being selected as a scholar, and more importantly, at just having a better overall experience win or not.

Part II focuses on serving students both broadly and effectively. Karna Walter (University of Arizona) in "Student Engagement: A Road to Travel More" discusses the importance of the multiple purposes—both public and private—of higher education to fellowships advisors. Advisors work to help students achieve their potential and in many ways to serve the public good. Walter stresses the importance of students reflecting on their engagement experiences, encouraging scholarship advisors to reach out to offices where this kind of experiential learning is taking place. Students who have been involved in engaged learning may have a better sense of direction and are more likely to be developing long-term goals and plans. And they may be ready to apply for scholarships that have the potential to help realize those plans. By knowing the engaged learning landscape on the campus and in the community, advisors can be advocates for these experiences. They can also create partnerships that allow them to discover students who have had experiences that make them good prospects for particular awards.

Gihan Fernando, the executive director of American University's career center, also reflects on partnerships in "Scholarships as a Pathway to Government Service." He makes a persuasive case in chapter 6 that career centers can be excellent partners with scholarship advising offices especially when assisting students who are planning careers in governmental service. Career centers as a matter of course help students identify their strengths and their main interests, and they are usually more familiar with government internships and opportunities. Collaborating with such a center as an advisor guides a student through a scholarship application can be very helpful—both as professional development for the advisor and as individual support for a given student. Fernando also provides excellent advice on obtaining security clearances for students who have internship opportunities with the government, and he discusses in detail the Presidential Management Program, a main entry-level program for working in the federal government.

Though most fellowships advisors do not spend a lot of time advising on general study abroad programs, they can be asked by students who frequent their offices for advice, and advisors certainly want students who have studied abroad to be thoughtful about that experience as they apply for nationally competitive awards. Many advisors already partner with study abroad offices on scholarships like the DAAD, Gilman, Boren, and Fulbright, and they may have some familiarity with the programs offered by their own campuses. In chapter 7, Richard Montauk provides advice on how to assist students as they think about the possibility of studying abroad. The guide does not intend to be an exhaustive manual or to transform someone into an expert study abroad advisor, but it does provide helpful overall information for fellowships advisors and includes a vocabulary that advisors will find useful when having a productive conversation with a student who is hoping to go abroad or one who has just returned.

Doug Cutchins (New York University, Abu Dhabi), David Schug (University of Illinois at Urbana-Champaign), and Mary Denyer (Marshall Aid Commemoration Commission) combine forces in chapter 8 to provide an in-depth look at writing letters of endorsement, a genre that differs in nuanced ways from standard letters of recommendation. In "Bela Karolyi's Handstand: The Whys and Hows of Letters of Endorsement," the authors review various scholarships that require endorsement, highlighting different expectations. The essay is a lively look at how advisors become part of the equation in this aspect of the application, and after addressing the *whys*, it provides sound advice on the *hows*, including how to gain information from the student that translates to a persuasive narrative, how to know what to include and what not to include, how to avoid gender-biased language, and how to decide who will sign the institution's letter.

The essays in part III focus on expanding opportunities in very specific ways. Chapters 9 and 10 address issues of diversity. In chapter 9, Jennifer Gerz-Escandón examines how advisors can broaden their application pools to include students from underrepresented groups. The varying degree of difficulty in doing so depends on campus demographics. At some institutions, it can be more challenging. Gerz-Escandón places the drive to increase diversity into historical and scholarship foundation contexts. She then relies on institutions that have devised creative and successful identification and recruitment plans to show the way. Lessons are gleaned from Perimeter College in Atlanta (first-generation and nontraditional students), Salisbury State in Maryland (faculty involvement), University of California, Berkeley (community college outreach), and University of Southern Florida in Tampa (satellite campus outreach to Pell and minority students). Many of the suggestions are practical and implementation is straightforward, serving as a guide to institutions looking to expand access.

In chapter 10, Brandy Simula, a trained sociologist from Emory University, continues the discussion on diversity, taking the student perspective. In "Belonging, Impostor Phenomenon, and Advising Students from Underrepresented Backgrounds," Simula analyzes what it means for students to feel like they belong and how elusive that sense of belonging can be for some students from underrepresented backgrounds. A diverse group of students may be hard to recruit for scholarships or awards because they may not see themselves as belonging in that cohort, and advising offices may unwittingly contribute to their sense of being outsiders. Simula provides practical advice for evaluating whether or not an office is welcoming to diverse groups, for reaching out to underrepresented communities, and for communicating with students once they have decided to apply.

The final essay in this part focuses on the Benjamin A. Gilman International Scholarship, a need-based (Pell required), merit-worthy aid for talented students from low-income backgrounds to study abroad. Barbara Stedman (Ball State University) dedicates a significant portion of her staff's time to the Gilman Scholarship and was curious if other benchmark institutions did the same. She discovered that for the bulk of the institutions she queried, the office of study abroad manages the Gilman program for the institution, but many fellowships advisors indicated they work collaboratively with the office. And the exclamatory "Thank goodness for Gilman" from one advisor resonated with many. Most offices put in significant amounts of time for this award because the benefit to the students is so great.

The collection ends with part IV, "On the Profession." In chapter 12, Lauren Tuckley (Georgetown University) calls for members of NAFA to investigate advising issues through a rigorous research lens that includes literature-based, data-driven analyses. Her study "Writing Self-Efficacy in Postsecondary Fellowship Applicants: The Relationship between Two Types of Feedforward Treatments" is offered as an example. In the study, Tuckley asks interesting questions about students' understanding of their writing abilities and the role the advisor plays in developing that understanding. She makes clear the need for additional research on this and other topics.

In the final essay, "Reflections on the Value of Being in the Room Where It Happens," Elizabeth Vardaman contemplates what it meant for her to be a founding member of NAFA. She divides her assessment into two sections: then and now. The headiness of the early years of helping launch a successful national and international enterprise gives way to the more life-sustaining work at home. Having been part of those early NAFA discussions, she has been invited to many game-changing conversations on her campus. Vardaman provides insights on how members of NAFA can translate the expertise they develop through their work and through the organization into new and persuasive conversations across their campuses. She quotes Nancy Twiss, a much admired (and long retired) advisor from Kansas State University, "As the years passed, we saw that the University could help candidates, but we had not expected the reverse: that our nominees and the application process would affect the intellectual climate of the University." For Baylor, and perhaps for other institutions, this has been or will be the case as well.

Scholarship foundations provide talented students with exceptional opportunities to expand and enhance their experiences and skills as they move to careers in which many will be leaders in their fields. Fellowships advisors are in a position to expand the benefits of these awards to a multitude of students beyond the "lucky few" who win by using applications as road maps for students to develop long-term goals and plans, to decide on or reflect about appropriate kinds of student engagement, and to determine an area where the student might be an agent for change. Students, advisors, and institutions who view outcomes with long-term academic and career objectives in mind will have a winning experience every time.

# Part I

## Foundations

# 1

# Public Service, Power, and the Challenges Facing Millennials

## ANDREW RICH

*Andrew Rich* *has been executive secretary of the Harry S. Truman Scholarship Foundation since 2011. He directs the independent federal agency that provides merit-based Truman Scholarships to college students who plan to attend graduate school in preparation for careers in public service. Before joining the Truman Foundation, Rich was president and CEO of the Roosevelt Institute, a nonprofit organization devoted to carrying forward the legacy and values of Franklin and Eleanor Roosevelt. Rich is the author of* Think Tanks, Public Policy, and the Politics of Expertise *(Cambridge University Press, 2004), as well as a wide-ranging number of articles on the role of experts and ideas in the American policy process. He was chair of the Political Science Department at the City College of New York (CCNY) before joining the Roosevelt Institute. From 1999 to 2003, he taught political science at Wake Forest University. He received his BA from the University of Richmond and his PhD in political science from Yale University. He was a 1991 Truman Scholar from Delaware.*

**A** well-functioning society requires effective public servants. They are the people who teach our children and keep our children healthy. They build our roads and our spacecraft. They protect our people and our planet. They are scientists and soldiers, social workers and city planners, grassroots activists and elected officials. They are first responders in emergencies and the last people defending our rights. Public service is tough; it is often unglamorous. But it is essential.[1]

As a society, we are off on the wrong track in so many ways in supporting and encouraging public service—on the wrong track for public servants who want to make a difference in politics and government, in particular. This has happened, especially over the past thirty-five years, in ways that smart, ambitious young people perceive. As a result, too often millennials do not view public service—and especially government—as a way to make a positive difference. Too few of the best aspire to it. If we do not turn this trend around, we risk having too many of the wrong kinds of people in public service—those who misunderstand power and how to make change. Or perhaps understand it too well but do not intend to use it for purposes that improve society.

The national fellowships community provides an important line of defense against this problem. We make a difference in affecting the career paths of talented and ambitious young people. All of us have the chance to engage students at a particularly crucial moment in their professional development around questions of power, politics, service, and democracy. Doing that in ways that encourage outstanding young people to consider and see the value of careers in public service is an exciting and essential project.

## Millennials and Public Service

By all accounts, the challenges facing our country are enormous, and by most accounts, our political institutions and leaders are ill-equipped to address them. This is not a political or ideological point. Rather, this is an observation about the weakness of our political institutions. On the one hand, most institutions were created for particular purposes in the twentieth century, and they have had difficulty adapting to the needs and concerns of the twenty-first century. On the other hand, there is an assessment of our political leaders in both parties, who too often seem polarized, incapable of action, and beholden to special interests.

The problems in our politics run deep. They took decades to create, and these are conditions that will take time for us to improve. At the end of the day, I am optimistic about what is possible, however, because I think millennials have much to offer if they can figure out how to connect their ambitions to public service.

Admittedly, on first blush, millennials give us plenty of reason to worry. The complaints about their generation are well documented. They appear to have an increased sense of entitlement. They are attached—all the time—by their thumbs to their phones, and they are often not very adept at establishing real human connections. While there is evidence for these claims, when it comes to public service, millennials might just be our hope.

Research suggests that millennials are a "civic" generation. They are group-oriented, problem-solving, institution builders or, in other words, a "we" generation. Millennials engage in community service at much higher rates than previous generations; this is especially true for those who attend college. In 2014, 88 percent of college freshmen reported that they had participated in community service in high school, and 60 percent of those graduating from college indicated that they want to engage in service to "help the country." A Pew survey indicates that 58 percent of millennials had "done volunteer activities through or for an organization" within the previous year.[2]

So what is the problem? It has to do with how millennials engage civically compared with previous generations. They are not voting—at least not at the rates of previous generations when they were young. Millennials made up 19 percent of the 2012 electorate. In 2016, they represented 31 percent of the electorate—as big a part of the electorate as baby boomers. In 2016, only 50 percent of millennials voted, less than older generations.[3]

With respect to their careers, millennials want to engage in different ways. They think about power and freedom (and risk) differently from older generations. They are not attracted to working in the public service institutions—government and the nonprofit sector—that their parents and grandparents created. Many have little interest in politics, as such. Many are not particularly interested in Washington, D.C. In fact, they are often distrustful of Washington. They identify less often as partisan—at least in the ways that older Americans might categorize themselves as Democrats or Republicans. They are civically minded as problem solvers, concerned with issues, and quite often, concerned either at the transnational level or at the local level.

Every year, I spend the month of March on the road for Truman finalist interviews. I participate in 200 interviews, and a career goal we hear a lot is social entrepreneurship: the desire to accomplish social goals—and make society better—through the methods of the private sector. Candidates see more possibility for impact through entrepreneurship than government, and they are attracted to the possibilities for immediate, measurable results that social entrepreneurship claims to provide. While perhaps fine for some, this preference misses key opportunities for millennials to engage the institutions of government, in particular—where the greatest power resides and where change can be scaled for the largest numbers to benefit.

## The Challenges of Public Service

So what is going on here? Evidence suggests that millennials have sized up the world that their parents have handed them, and they are making some reasonable judgments about what is possible and where best to expend their energy. The orienting event for millennials when it comes to civic engagement is 9/11 and its aftermath. For those drawn to public service, it is a defining event, and for many it is *the* defining event from their childhood that has set the stage for so much that has come since. Millennials have grown up in the midst of two wars; during Truman interviews, I am frequently reminded that millennials cannot remember a time when the United States was not at war. In addition, they and their families experienced the deep recession of 2008—the collapse of the housing market and the financial sector. They have lived through a slow recovery, one in which millennials have experienced the disproportionate effects of youth unemployment, which remains in double digits at just more than 10 percent.[4]

Then, they look at government, and they see sclerosis—inaction, polarization, and corruption. Young people have a hard time naming domestic political figures whom they admire. They are distressed by the role of money in politics and the disproportionate influence of lobbyists. They do not see political institutions working effectively, and they do not see them as a way to address the problems that animate their interests in public service.

All of this is reinforced by dominant narratives in the United States that bolster a distrust of government. For many, these narratives are as influential as reality. I spent much of the early part of my career studying the "war of ideas" in American politics—the growth of a free-market, conservative movement, in particular, that succeeded at discrediting government. This movement reshaped the point of departure in public and policy discussions so that government is seldom perceived as an effective vehicle for constructive change.

In the end, young people, by and large, have not experienced government in positive ways. And they have not been witness to or participants in movements that demonstrate how government can be successful. And so young people who are civically minded are thinking about public service in different ways. The bad news—at least I fear—is that all of this drives good young people away.

Combine everything that I have just described with the well-honed systems of private sector job recruitment that exist on many campuses, and it becomes no surprise that some of the most talented young people— including those who want to "make a difference"—become susceptible to the relentless and sophisticated recruitment efforts of Silicon Valley, management consulting firms, and Wall Street. Last summer, applications for summer positions with Goldman Sachs from college students and recent college graduates were at record levels. Goldman Sachs received almost 250,000 applications for summer employment—a 46 percent increase over 2012.[5] These young people, at least in surveys, indicate in overwhelming numbers that they want to have careers that make a difference. But they do not see government—or even nonprofits—as the way to do it.

## The Path Forward among Millennials

So I worry—especially about how the current realities and perceptions of public service affect those who might aspire to it. I worry because the belief that millennials can make change through the institutions of capitalism rather than democracy misunderstands some key possibilities around the effective exercise of power in our society. Fundamentally, for democracy to work, we have to engage government, including Washington, where so much power resides. We need young people to engage government. They have to understand and grapple with how change on a broad-based scale requires the power that can only be found in government. Millennials certainly do not need to share a view of government's appropriate role, but they have to engage government in serious ways.

I worry, but I am optimistic. Those of us who are a little older have made something of a mess of our politics and our institutions of public service. But there is growing evidence that some portion of millennials wants to fix things. They just want to do it, perhaps quite rationally, by challenging our institutions from the outside. We are knee deep in a movement for immigration reform in this country, and millennials are at the front, driving it from the outside. Millennials are leaders in building movements and organizing for change on a wide range of issues and on all sides of politics. While there is growing evidence that millennials may not be immediately attracted to traditional public service institutions, they are interested in challenging the power of these institutions from the outside, from both the right and the left—and from new angles and perspectives.

The Truman Foundation aims to support this work, and all of us in the national fellowships community can encourage it among outstanding young people. At Truman, we are attracted to candidates who have an analysis of how power operates to scale change and progress within our society. We look for candidates who would like to use power to make change—whether by challenging systems of power from the outside or aspiring to accumulate power within institutions. Our vision is a country that deeply values the diverse and innovative ways that Americans make a positive difference in the lives of others through public service.

President Truman once defined courage as "not always facing the foe, but in taking care of those at home with a true heart and a strong mind." Today we too often think of courage in political terms and taking a stand against a party or a policy. Millennials often have a different vision, and I think President Truman would approve. For what is needed is more courage to take bold chances, try new things, and explore new approaches. "The buck stops here" is Truman's most famous line. It speaks to accountability and the need to see a job done, whether that was getting a road built, the military desegregated, or rebuilding postwar Europe. This is no different today, with pressing challenges ranging from crumbling infrastructure to combating climate change and ISIS. The best public servants are steadfast in their determination to make a difference through deeds not words. They must act with an understanding of and a resolve to engage power and institutions.

At the end of the day, I am cautiously optimistic that millennials might help us get to a better place in our politics. By end of the decade, millennials will represent one in three voters. They are currently ambivalent about government and our political parties. But my hope—and I think there is some evidence to back this up—is that they will remake them. And I think that millennials may remake our understandings of politics in the process.

## Notes

1. This essay is adapted from a talk given at the Summer 2016 NAFA Regional Conference in Washington, D.C., "Public Service and Nationally Competitive Scholarships—Government, Social Activism, Research and Advocacy." The views expressed are those of the author and do not represent any institutional positions by the Truman Foundation.

2. Pew Research Center, March 2014, "Millennials in Adulthood: Detached from Institutions, Networked with Friends."

3. Matthew Green, "How Millennials Voted in the 2016 Presidential Election," *KQED News*, November 15, 2016.

4. "Monthly Unemployment Rate in the United States from December 2015 to December 2016," Statista, the Statistics Portal.

5. Emily Jane Fox, "Suddenly, Millennials Are Dying to Work on Wall Street Again," The Hive, *Vanity Fair*, June 6, 2016.

# 2

# The Goldwater Scholarship Program
Yesterday, Today, and Tomorrow

## JOHN MATEJA

*John Mateja* *became the third president of the Barry Goldwater Scholarship and Excellence in Education Foundation in January 2016. Mateja earned his BS in physics and PhD in nuclear physics from the University of Notre Dame in 1972 and 1976, respectively. He has held faculty and administrative positions at Tennessee Technological University and Murray State University and administrative positions at Argonne National Laboratory, Department of Energy, and the National Science Foundation. Throughout his career he has valued and advocated for the engagement of undergraduates in meaningful research experiences. He has held leadership positions in the Council on Undergraduate Research (CUR) for over thirty years, including serving as CUR president in 1993. He also served on the Board of Governors for the National Conference on Undergraduate Research (NCUR) prior to its merger with CUR and continues to serve in an oversight position. Mateja was named a Fellow of the American Physical Society and of the Council on Undergraduate Research for the work he has done to help change undergraduate education nationally.*

On the occasion of his retirement from the Senate in 1986, Congress created the Barry Goldwater Scholarship and Excellence in Education Foundation as a tribute to the leadership and vision of Senator Goldwater. The purpose of the foundation and its scholarship program is to ensure the nation has a continuing supply of well-prepared individuals who are pursuing research careers in the natural sciences, mathematics, and engineering. College undergraduates who are in either their sophomore or junior years of college are the sole focus of the scholarship program. Approximately 300 students are supported annually, with each student receiving a scholarship of up to $7,500. Details associated with the Goldwater application and selection process have been presented in an earlier publication by John A. Lanning and W. Franklin Gilmore.[1]

This year marks the thirtieth anniversary of the establishment of the Goldwater Foundation and, as the first scholarships were awarded in 1989, the twenty-seventh year the scholarships have been continuously awarded. Each year, approximately 2,000 colleges and universities identify a Goldwater Campus Representative who then coordinates their on-campus competitions, with each academic institution able to nominate up to four students. From 2013 to 2016, an average of 420 schools out of the 2,000 schools with campus representatives have nominated students annually.

From 1989 to the present, 7,681 students have been named Goldwater Scholars and have received over $61 million in scholarship support. Goldwater Scholars have come from over 600 academic institutions that represent all fifty states, the Commonwealth of Puerto Rico, and, as a sole entry, Guam, U.S. Virgin Islands, American Samoa, Commonwealth of Northern Marianas, and Trust Territories of the Pacific Islands.

To understand the larger impact of the Goldwater program, in 2014, then Goldwater president Frank Gilmore, at the request of the foundation's board of trustees, contracted with Washington State University's Social and Economic Sciences Research Center (SESRC) to survey the 6,975 students who had received scholarships from 1989 to 2013.[2] The purpose of the survey was to ask former scholars about their academic and professional careers. Useable contact information was available for 4,652 former Goldwater Scholars and, of these, 2,031 responded.[3]

Of considerable interest to the foundation is the number of scholars who obtained academic degrees and the level of those degrees. Of the 2,031 survey respondents, 98.6 percent reported that they had obtained at

**Table 2.1. Highest Academic Degree**

| Degree | Percentage |
|---|---|
| Bachelor's | 24.5 |
| Master's | 14.9 |
| PhD | 43.6 |
| MD/PhD | 4.7 |
| Medical (MD, DO, DDS, DVM) | 7.5 |
| Law (LLB or JD) | 0.8 |
| Other | 2.5 |
| Not Reported/Missing | 1.4 |
| TOTAL | 100 |

least one academic degree. Three individuals reported receiving six separate academic degrees and one reported seven degrees.

The survey asked about highest degree earned. The results, shown in Table 2.1, reveal that 24.5 percent have received a bachelor's degree, 14.9 percent have received a master's degree, 7.5 percent have received a medical degree, and nearly half—48.3 percent—have already received either a PhD (43.6 percent) or an MD-PhD (4.7 percent). At the time of the survey (2014), scholars who had received Goldwater awards from 2008 to 2013 had not yet had sufficient time to complete their doctoral degrees. Many of the scholars from this time period who had obtained their bachelor's and master's degrees were still working on their doctoral degrees. The total percentage of scholars who will ultimately attain a doctoral degree will likely approach 70 percent.

The survey went on to ask those who attained bachelor's, master's, and doctoral degrees for their highest-degree field of study (these are the scholars who did not indicate that they had obtained or were pursuing a medical or law degree). As seen in Table 2.2 and Figure 2.1, over 90 percent of the Goldwater Scholars fall into five major disciplinary areas: biology, chemistry, physics and astronomy, engineering, and mathematics. Approximately one-half of the awards over the past twenty-seven years have gone to students who have pursued research careers in biology or chemistry. The majority of the remaining 50 percent of the scholarships have been awarded to students majoring in physics and astronomy, engineering, and mathematics, with computer science, geo- and atmospheric sciences, and

## Table 2.2 Academic Discipline for the First Degree Earned

| Field | Percentage |
|---|---|
| Biology | 24 |
| Chemistry | 17 |
| Biochemistry | 9 |
| Physics and Astronomy | 17 |
| Mathematics | 11 |
| Engineering | 15 |
| Computer Science | 3 |
| Geo- and Atmospheric Sciences | 2 |
| Psychology | 1 |
| Other Fields | 1 |
| TOTAL | 100 |

## Figure 2.1. Distribution of Goldwater Scholars by Field of Study

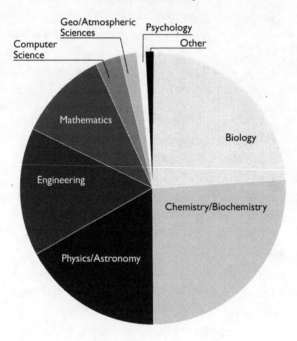

**Field of Study**

**Table 2.3. Number of Scholarships and Fellowships Awards**

| Awards/ Scholar | Frequency | Percentage | Awards/Scholar × Frequency |
|---|---|---|---|
| 0 | 942 | 47.1 | 0 |
| 1 | 513 | 25.7 | 513 |
| 2 | 356 | 17.8 | 712 |
| 3 | 127 | 6.4 | 381 |
| 4 | 38 | 1.9 | 144 |
| 5 | 17 | 0.9 | 85 |
| 6 | 0 | 0 | 0 |
| 7 | 4 | 0.2 | 28 |
| 8 | 0 | 0 | 0 |
| 9 | 2 | 0.1 | 18 |
| 10 | 1 | 0 | 10 |
| Total | 2000 | 100.0 | 1,891 |

psychology students sharing about 6 percent of the awards. Because the Goldwater Foundation has not kept or evaluated applicants' disciplinary data over the past twenty-seven years, it is impossible to determine the actual extent to which the number of awards simply tracked the applications. The nomination data, however, do still exist for the 2016 competition. Interestingly, one finds that 52 percent of the 2016 nominations are in biology and chemistry, suggesting that the number of awards likely does track closely with the number of students nominated in the different fields.

The survey went on to look at how Goldwater Scholars did in subsequent postgraduate scholarship competitions, such as Rhodes, Hertz, NSF Graduate Research Fellowship, Marshall, and Churchill. Fifty-two percent of the scholars report that they have won one or more additional awards and Table 2.3 shows the percentages for the number of additional scholarships Goldwater Scholars subsequently won. Of the over 2,000 scholars who responded to this question, collectively they won nearly 1,900 additional scholarships or fellowships.

Further mining of the survey data finds that Goldwater Scholars have won 624 National Science Foundation Graduate Research Fellowships, 55 Churchill Scholarships, 21 Fannie and John Hertz Foundation Scholarships, 133 NIH supported scholarships, 108 National Defense Science and

Engineering Graduate Fellowships, 39 Howard Hughes Medical Institute awards, 45 Marshall Scholarships, 40 Fulbright awards, and 21 Rhodes Scholarships, among others. These are truly remarkable achievements.

The Goldwater Foundation has kept accurate records over the past twenty-seven years on the number of awards all Goldwater Scholars have received for three national scholarships—Rhodes, Marshall, and Churchill. Through December 2016, Goldwater Scholars have gone on to win 86 Rhodes Scholarships, 127 Marshall Scholarships, and 134 Churchill Scholarships.

## Broader Impacts

While the data provide a statistical overview of the Goldwater program, this data, by itself, provide a limited insight into the program's human and institutional impacts. To obtain a better understanding of the program's impact in these areas, the foundation surveyed the more than 2,000 Goldwater Campus Representatives in early 2016 and began collecting vignettes on the Goldwater Scholars. While this information is anecdotal, it does help provide a window into the human and programmatic impacts the Goldwater Foundation has had on students, faculty, and institutions nationally.

The comments provided by the Goldwater Campus Representatives in the early 2016 survey suggest important impacts across many sectors of the university. Institutions clearly take considerable pride in the science, engineering, and mathematics students who win Goldwater Scholarships or receive an Honorable Mention. The Goldwater Campus Representatives report that their institutions (1) recognize Goldwater recipients at honors convocations and commencements, (2) celebrate them on their websites, (3) feature them in fundraising magazines, (4) invite them to meet with their regents, (5) highlight them in chancellor reports, (6) publicly display them on billboards, (7) display scholars' names on a campus "Scholar Walk" and in a permanent student union "Scholars Gallery," (8) mention their Goldwater Scholars in grant proposals, and (9) light a bell tower in their honor.

As the result of the Goldwater Scholarship, many campuses have increased their involvement with and support of undergraduate research. Comments like the following can be found throughout the 2016 survey:

"Our success in the Goldwater competition has inspired our students to engage in undergraduate research-based education," "The success of our students [with the Goldwater program] has helped create and foster a very strong, campus-wide culture of undergraduate research," "Knowing about the Goldwater Scholarship has enabled more of our freshman STEM (Science, Technology, Engineering, and Mathematics) majors to start doing research," "It has helped promote undergraduate research, particularly with women in STEM disciplines," and "We have a new emerging scholars program for freshmen in part to help groom candidates for the Goldwater."

Interestingly, many Goldwater Campus Representatives report that, win or lose, students benefited by going through the Goldwater nomination process. As one campus representative recount, "The students who do not win still build closer relationships with their professors and think more deeply about their goals within their academic discipline." Another campus representative describes the impact of the application process in this way, "The campus nomination competition is very tough but also extremely beneficial even for students who aren't nominated. We have had students who did not win the nomination go on to top ten PhD programs and win NSF Graduate Research Fellowships—in part, no doubt, because of the reflective process and letters of recommendation gained in the Goldwater application process in their sophomore and junior year." Finally, rather than discourage students about their future, not obtaining a Goldwater appears to encourage them. As one campus representative reports, "One of our current Goldwaters was turned down as a sophomore applicant. He told me after going through the process that he now understood what he needed to do to be a future leader in research. He went on to win a DAAD award for research in Germany, came back and won a Goldwater, and continues to reach for the stars." What appears to be clear from the Goldwater Campus Representatives' comments is that completing the application requires that undergraduates begin to "plan" their career paths, which, up until the point of completing the Goldwater application, they generally had not done. Another campus representative reports, "Students see the [Goldwater application] process as helping to develop them to write better about their aspirations and their science, and to help prepare them to develop applications for graduate school, federal fellowships, and other national/international scholarships."

For many students who win a Goldwater Scholarship, the financial impact of the award is critical. Stories like those of Dr. Matthew Evans ('96 Scholar) are common. Evans, who has spent much of his career working on the LIGO (Laser Interferometer Gravitational-Wave Observatory) project that recently verified the existence of gravitational waves, commented when asked about his Goldwater award, "For whatever reason, I naively expected that some form of financial aid would materialize when I arrived at Harvey Mudd to help me get by. The Goldwater award made a huge difference, and it is quite possible that without it, I would not have been able to finish my undergraduate degree." When she was being interviewed by a Pittsburgh TribLive reporter, 2016 Goldwater recipient Kara McClain from Indiana University of Pennsylvania said, "I was excited to win. I'm responsible for my own finances. So next year, I won't have to take any loans."[4] In McClain's eyes, next year should be easy! With no loan debt to worry about, she will only have to juggle twenty credits a semester with clinical work in a hospital, work on her Goldwater-winning research studying tick-borne diseases, and travel as the only competitive female member of the university's cycling team. Not only has the scholarship "lessened the financial worry" and enabled students to remain in school, it has broadened their opportunity to include study abroad. One recent Goldwater winner was able to participate in a comparative ecology study in Hungary and one added an international dimension to her study of the bee crisis through eight months of research in Argentina.

There are, of course, impacts of winning a Goldwater that go well beyond those that are financial. Many students are like first-generation college student, Paul Urayama, who attended the University of California, Irvine. They are in college simply because "it's the next thing to do." While Paul was fortunate to find a research opportunity as an undergraduate at Irvine with Professors Bill Heidbrink and Gregory Benford, it was not obvious at this point to Paul that doing research was an *actual* career possibility, not, at least, until he won a Goldwater in 1993. "Winning was a big deal" Paul would say when asked to reflect on receiving the award. "Without the Goldwater, I may not have realized that doing research—that, lifelong learning—was a *real* career option!" Winning the Goldwater was also instrumental in putting Paul on a path to a PhD in physics at Princeton University. Today Dr. Urayama is on the physics faculty at Miami University in Ohio. Throughout his professional career, Paul has and is giving back. He has mentored fifty-seven students, with two of his students winning Goldwater awards. Today, as Miami University's Goldwater Campus Representative, he is seeking out and working with undergraduates from across the university. Whether or not they win a Goldwater award, Dr. Urayama sees the application process as valuable "in honing the students' critical thinking skills, in helping them develop independent ideas, and, most importantly, in helping them dig deep to discover their passion for doing research."

The campus representatives who responded to the 2016 survey also reported that the Goldwater has had a significant impact on faculty. The campus representatives reported that "While the Goldwater process has its greatest impact on the applicants, it also contributes greatly to the collaborative and ambitious culture among our science faculty," "The Scholarship has made science faculty look more closely at our promising student researchers and bring them to a higher level of achievement," "[Our faculty] take great pride in their Goldwater Scholars who have gone on to become top researchers and faculty in their turn," and "[The faculty] start to view undergraduate research as being an essential part of their curriculum."

The Goldwater Campus Representatives further related that they view the Goldwater application as the "ideal template for mapping a student's interests, goals and plans to succeed" and that it gives them the "opportunity to work with students and teach them how to proofread and edit their written work."

At the institutional level, Goldwater scholarships are frequently cited as "bringing prestige and honor to the University," "being an important recruitment tool," "providing prestige and promotion for the excellent departments in which the students study and work," and "helping raise an institution's profile among its peer schools." One institution credited its Goldwater recipients as being responsible for much of its external grant success: "Much of the $5.7 million in grant funding that we have received over the years was, according to the proposal reviews, a direct result of our success in the Goldwater competition." Then, of course, there is the good-natured academic rivalry the Goldwater Scholarship appears to promote among institutions. More than one Goldwater Campus Representative indicated that their institution takes pride in having "more Goldwater Scholars than any other school in our region."

## What's New for 2017?

The most apparent changes to the Goldwater program over the past year have been to the Goldwater website and to the Goldwater online application. Working with a team of web developers and web designers from Scholarship America,[5] both the website and the online application have been completely revamped. To ensure that all undergraduates have the opportunity to make their interest in competing for a Goldwater Scholarship known to their institution's Goldwater Campus Representative and to track the number of these students, a new pre-application was added to the Goldwater online nomination process. When submitted, the pre-application is forwarded to the institution's Goldwater Campus Representative. Upon review of the pre-application, the campus representative can provide the student with immediate access to the full online application; schedule a one-on-one meeting with the student to further review the student's credentials; or reject the pre-application, citing the reasons for rejection. An important new focus of the Goldwater website is that it now celebrates our scholars and their many achievements. Vignettes of current and former scholars, being written by our Goldwater Campus Representatives or, in many cases, written collaboratively by a campus representative and the former scholar, are now being posted on the Goldwater website and Facebook page.

The online nomination process has also been substantially modified. The new site puts much of the control of the application process in the hands of the Goldwater Campus Representative. In addition to making the decision on the students' pre-applications, the responsibility for setting all campus deadlines now rests with the campus representatives. The final submission deadline—5:00 p.m. Central Time on the last Friday in January—is the only deadline the foundation now sets. The campus representative, for example, establishes the internal deadlines for receipt of the students' applications and reference letters. Other changes to the Goldwater nomination process include (1) all two- and four-year schools, can now nominate up to four students, (2) both "official" and "unofficial" transcripts may be submitted, (3) all ancillary materials can now be uploaded as PDF files (supporting materials are no longer mailed to the foundation), and (4) adoption of the NSF's Graduate Research Fellows Fields of Study, better aligning the Goldwater and the NSF GRF applications.

The Goldwater award is about recognizing and celebrating the success of students, their mentors, and the institutions that foster this success. While the foundation has listed the names of the students who have won awards and included the names of these students' institutions on our website, this information does not provide much insight into how these students got to be where they are today. There is generally always a supportive environment created by faculty and others like the campus representatives that has helped a student achieve success. Three years ago Goldwater president Frank Gilmore and Beth Ambos, the executive director of the Council on Undergraduate Research (CUR), recognized that faculty mentors were not being acknowledged for their contributions to the students' success. Gilmore and Ambos were the impetus behind creating the CUR-Goldwater Scholar Faculty Mentor award. Three outstanding mentors—Francis Connelly (mathematics), University of Notre Dame; Bruce Jackson (biotechnology), MassBay Community College; and Carol Parish (chemistry), University of Richmond—have been selected for the award thus far. Their inspiring stories can be found on the Goldwater web page (https://goldwater.scholarsapply.org/faculty-mentors/). Both the Goldwater Foundation and CUR encourage academic institutions to nominate faculty who have outstanding records working with Goldwater Scholars on their campuses for this important recognition.

In terms of recognizing the faculties' contributions to students winning a Goldwater award, creating the faculty mentor award was certainly a step in the right direction. However, there are hundreds of faculty, and also Goldwater Campus Representatives, who should be acknowledged for their efforts in helping our scholars achieve success. Starting in 2017, all faculty mentors and campus representatives of students who receive Goldwater Scholarships or Honorable Mentions will be listed on the foundation's web page along with their students.

For the first time in 2016, the foundation informed several scientific professional societies that students in their disciplinary areas had been recognized for their meritorious achievements by the Goldwater Foundation. Recipients of Goldwater awards are clearly the kind of students these societies want to attract to their memberships. To this end, the American Physical Society (APS) sent congratulatory letters and a free year's APS membership to all undergraduate physics and astronomy Goldwater recipients.

In summary, the Goldwater Scholarship and Excellence in Education Foundation has thus far provided 7,681 undergraduates with over $61 million in scholarship support and has been an important driving factor in changing the way undergraduates are educated in the United States. Upward of 70 percent of the Goldwater scholarship recipients have in turn gone on to earn PhDs in their chosen fields and are today among the country's scientific, engineering, and mathematics leaders. As important, the individuals who were once student Goldwater Scholars are now—and will be into the foreseeable future—the mentors for the country's next generation of science, engineering, and mathematics talent.

## Notes

1. John A. Lanning and W. Franklin Gilmore, "Expanding Undergraduate Research Opportunities: Goldwater Scholarships in Mathematics, Science and Engineering," *All In: Expanding Access Through Nationally Competitive Awards,* edited by Suzanne McCray (Fayetteville: University of Arkansas Press, 2013), 33–42.

2. The author would like to thank former Goldwater president, Frank Gilmore, and the foundation's executive administrator, Lucy Decher, for all the work they did to make the 2014 scholar survey possible. They spent countless hours obtaining current contact information on our Goldwater Scholars.

3. Social and Economic Sciences Research Center (SESRC), Data Report 15–006, Washington State University, Pullman, WA, 2015.

4. Debra Erdley, "Western Pa. Goldwater Scholarship Winners Encouraged to Further Research," *Tribune-Review,* http://triblive.com/state/pennsylvania /10314804–74/research-goldwater-university.

5. Scholarship America, https://scholarshipamerica.org/.

# 3

# The James Madison Memorial Fellowship Foundation
*Transforming Outstanding Undergraduates into Teachers of the Constitution*

## CLAIRE MCCAFFERY GRIFFIN

---

*Claire McCaffery Griffin is an independent consultant with more than forty years of experience in civic education. A Madison Fellow from the first class of fellows (1992), she currently works with the James Madison Memorial Fellowship Foundation as its director of special projects, coordinating outreach, publications, and programs. She earned her BA degree at the University of San Francisco and MA degree from the University of Hawaii at Manoa. She was a high school teacher for twenty-eight years and then served as vice president of Education Programs for the Bill of Rights Institute, where she edited or coauthored eight curricular resources, for example,* The Bill of Rights and You *and* Media and American Democracy, *and presented professional development programs to thousands of teachers from all fifty states. Since 2010, she has been an independent consultant working with nonprofits and government agencies to promote civic education. She is the coeditor of* Roots of Liberty: Unlocking the Federalist Papers *and coauthor of* Communism: Its Ideology, Its History, and Its Legacy.

---

> If you want to be a better teacher of the Constitution, apply for the James Madison Memorial Fellowship. If you want to challenge your knowledge and opinions concerning the Constitution, apply for the fellowship. If you want to be competitive in the field of education, apply for the fellowship. If you want to study the Constitution with top academics in the field and with fellow teachers from across the country, apply for the fellowship.

These comments from Matthew Burgoyne, a 2015 Madison Fellow from Washington, D.C., currently pursuing graduate studies at American University, eloquently summarize the purpose, value, and prestige of the James Madison Memorial Fellowship.[1] The James Madison Memorial Fellowship Foundation was established by Congress in 1986 for the purpose of improving teaching about the U.S. Constitution in secondary schools. These fellowships honor the legacy of James Madison by providing support for graduate study for teachers (both pre-service and in-service) that focuses on the Constitution—its history and contemporary relevance to the practices and policies of democratic government.

The benefits of the fellowship program are manifold and lasting for both the fellows and the nation. Emily Lake, a 2016 fellow from New Jersey, holds a BA from the University of Texas and is studying at the University of Chicago. She stresses, "The fellowship will help prepare recipients to be better teachers by growing content knowledge on a critical piece of our nation's history—constitutional history. It is more important now than ever for our high school students to have a comprehensive understanding of the Constitution, its development, and its applications to the present day. Our students will be the next generation of scholars, political leaders, or Supreme Court justices making major decisions about constitutional law. Educating these young people on the Constitution begins with educating their teachers."

Since the program's inception in 1992, nearly 1,400 fellowships have been awarded, and 85.8 percent of all fellows have completed (or are in the process of completing) their academic programs and teaching obligations. Fellows have taught more than two million students and are regularly recognized for their commitment to student excellence. Madison Fellows serve as state and district supervisors, play active roles in their communities, and nearly forty fellows teach full- or part-time in the history, political science, education, or law departments of community colleges and universities. John B. King Jr., a New Jersey fellow from the class of 1995, served as U.S. Secretary of Education under President Barack Obama, and the current president of the National Council for the Social Studies, Peggy Jackson, is a 2002 fellow from New Mexico.

To be eligible to apply for a fellowship, individuals must

- be a U.S. citizen or U.S. national;
- be a teacher, or plan to become a teacher, of American history, American government, or civics at the secondary school level (grades 7–12); and
- possess a bachelor's degree or plan to receive a bachelor's degree no later than August 31 of the year in which they are applying.

Applicants must be committed to teaching American history, American government, or any other social studies class where they will teach topics on the Constitution full-time in grades 7–12, and qualify for admission with graduate standing at an accredited U.S. university.

The fellowships support graduate study leading to a master's degree. James Madison Fellows may attend any accredited institution of higher education in the United States, including schools outside of their state of residence, and have matriculated at nearly 400 institutions since the program was begun in 1992. Each fellow is expected to pursue and complete a master's degree in one of the following fields:

- Master of Arts (MA) in American history, political science, or government.
- Master of Arts in Teaching (MAT) concentrating on either American Constitutional history (in a history department) or American government, political institutions, or political theory

(in a political science department). MAT degrees without required
constitutional coursework cannot be approved.
- Master of Education (MEd) or the Master of Arts or Master of
  Science in Education with a concentration in American history or
  American government, political institutions, and political theory.

Whatever the degree selected, the program must award credit for at least
twelve semester hours or their equivalent for study of the origins, principles, and development of the U.S. Constitution. Examples of constitutional content courses include constitutional history, legal history, or political science courses in federalism, presidency, Congress, the judiciary,
American political thought, and political and legal philosophy.

An independent Fellowship Selection Committee, composed of university faculty and James Madison Fellows who have completed their
teaching obligation, evaluates all valid applications submitted by the annual deadline. Applications are due March 1 of each year, and award letters are sent in late April.

The number of fellowships awarded is determined by the amount of
funding (from government sources or from private donations) available in
any given year. The goal of the foundation is to award one fellowship per
state per year. Applicants compete *only* against other applicants from the
state of their legal residence and are evaluated on their demonstrated commitment to a career teaching American history, American government,
or civics; their demonstrated intent to pursue and complete a program of
graduate study that emphasizes the Constitution and offers instruction
in that subject, their demonstrated devotion to civic responsibility, their
demonstrated capacity for study and performance as teachers, and their
proposed courses of graduate study.

The application (available at www.JamesMadison.gov) is quite extensive, requiring several short essays, one lengthy essay on the Constitution, and several letters of reference. The foundation offers suggestions for
preparing an exemplary application (https://goo.gl/i0brDy) since a well
thought-out and reviewed application is key to being awarded a James
Madison Fellowship. There are no personal interviews for this fellowship;
the application stands on its own.

There are two types of fellowships that recognize the different challenges and circumstances between those without teaching experience and those currently teaching. Junior Fellowships are awarded to outstanding college seniors and college graduates without teaching experience who intend to become secondary schoolteachers of American history, American government, or civics in grades 7–12. Senior Fellowships are awarded to outstanding current teachers. Applicants for both types of fellowships compete against each other in their respective states and fellowship type.

Applicants for Junior Fellowships may be concerned that they are not competitive with seasoned and experienced educators. However, the selection committee members have been successful in discerning the potential of pre-service teachers. Each year, approximately 20–25 percent of all applications are from pre-service teachers, and each year, the selection committee awards 20–25 percent of all fellowships to pre-service teachers. This is neither a quota nor a coincidence, but rather the result of an equitable evaluation of all applications. Since 1992, 1,353 fellowships have been awarded and 22 percent of those (300) have been awarded to recent graduates (Junior Fellows).

Sara Gittleman, a 2015 fellow from New Jersey with a BA from Rutgers, who is currently studying at the University of Nebraska, notes that junior applicants should "prepare applications in advance and maintain a positive attitude. Unlike the Senior Fellows, Junior Fellows are not experienced teachers. By applying early, they can start to prepare for this challenge. They can watch teachers, ask what they are doing well, and what they could do to improve. Junior Fellow applicants have the advantage of being able to adopt the perspective of both the student and the teacher. They should not perceive themselves as being inexperienced or at a disadvantage. Instead, they should take advantage of the familiarity with both roles, which will allow them to be even more approachable and open-minded educators."

Those sentiments are echoed by Caitlin Halperin, a 2015 fellow from Alabama who holds a BA and an MA from Auburn University: "If applicants are coming from an undergraduate program, I would recommend students rely on their methods courses to explain their philosophy of teaching. While Junior Fellow applicants do not have as much experience in the classroom, I encourage them to include as many experiences as they have (through practicums, student teaching) that illustrate their teaching philosophy, as well."

Upon receipt of the award, Junior Fellows must complete graduate study within two academic years of full-time study. They are expected to begin their teaching career upon receipt of their master's degree. The foundation does not function as a job-placement service for these new educators, but a combination of their talent, the foundation's LinkedIn group, and the networking available to them as fellows helps to ensure prompt job placement. "I am about to finish my Master's program at Villanova and am currently looking for a job. Already, I am noticing the difference that saying, 'I'm a James Madison Fellow,' makes for my search process. In the education realm, the title is prestigious," confirmed Joey Landgraf, a 2015 fellow who holds a BA from the University of Maryland and an MA from Villanova.

Each fellow must teach American history, American government, or any other social studies class that includes constitutional topics in grades 7–12 for one full year for each academic year of aid received, preferably in the state from which the recipient won the fellowship. Generally, Junior Fellows have a one- or two-year teaching commitment, but the vast majority of them (nearly 85 percent) become career educators.

The maximum amount of each award is $24,000, prorated over the period of study. In no case will the award exceed $12,000 for one academic year of study. Normally, fellows receive less than these maximum amounts. Payments are made only for the actual costs of tuition, required fees, books, and room and board, and are made only for the minimum number of credits required.

Each fellow must make satisfactory progress toward the degree and remain in good academic standing, completing the graduate degree of study within the expected amount of time. Junior Fellows may not be engaged in gainful employment that interferes with the fellow's studies. In addition to coursework at their universities, fellows are required, during the term of the fellowship, to attend the foundation's Summer Institute. The four-week Summer Institute is held each summer in Washington, D.C., on the campus of Georgetown University, and housing, meals, books, and travel costs are covered by the fellowship. The core of the Institute is a challenging graduate course, "The Foundations of American Constitutionalism," which provides six units of credit toward the fellows' degrees. In addition to the graduate coursework, participants have the opportunity to visit historic sites associated with the institutions of American government and the Constitution's framers.

This "constitutional boot camp" is a bonding experience shared by all fellows and ensures that each of them has the same essential understanding of constitutional principles, regardless of their specific course of study at their home university. As Sara Gittleman notes, "The Summer Institute was truly a once-in-a-lifetime experience, and is certainly a conversation starter. It is what makes this fellowship unique. No one else in my department spent their summer engaged in a conversation with U.S. Secretary of Education John B. King Jr., speaking with Associate Supreme Court Justice Anthony Kennedy, or listening to Senators Ben Cardin (D-MD) or John Cornyn III (R-TX). Those were opportunities that I had because I was fortunate enough to be named a James Madison Fellow."

In recent years, the foundation has made a concerted effort to recruit more Junior Fellows. We have revised our print publications to include more traditional college-age faces; we have dramatically increased our social media presence; and we sent letters and brochures to various departments (history, political science, education, honors, financial aid) at nearly 1,700 colleges and universities.

However, fellowships advisors can play a key role in publicizing the James Madison Memorial Fellowship. In a recent survey of Junior Fellows, numerous fellows reported that the prestigious fellowships coordinator (or a similar individual) made them aware of the fellowship. Tim McCall, a 2010 fellow from New Jersey with a BA from Bates College and an MA from the University of Connecticut, reports, "I first heard about the Madison Fellowship when I was working with the Grants and Fellowships Advisor, Dr. Sagaree Sangupta, while she coached me through a Fulbright application. She mentioned the Madison Fellowship in passing, when I expressed my hope to pursue further graduate work in American history. I ultimately received the Fulbright Fellowship, and while living in Germany, I applied to graduate schools. When considering how to pay for my graduate education, I recalled the Madison Fellowship. I reached out to Sagaree and she offered me some feedback on my application as I worked on it over in Germany."

Fellowships advisors can also network with their colleagues in the history, political science, and education departments. Adam Krauss, a 2010 fellow from New Hampshire with a BA from Suffolk University and an

MA from the University of New Hampshire, suggests, "When it comes to spreading the word about the fellowship, I think social media and other newfangled strategies certainly have their place but face-to-face contact still works pretty well. So, pop into classes, make a pitch, leave some information, and take some questions. Of course, let them know the fellowship not only provides astronomical financial benefits helping pay for graduate school but also links them with an entire universe of civic-minded educators from across the land."

Unlike other federal programs funding graduate school education, the James Madison Fellowship does not require applicants to have a faculty sponsor or nominator—anyone can apply and there can be an unlimited number of applications from each college or university. Nonetheless, faculty members and fellowships advisors can certainly mentor, encourage, nudge, and nag potential applicants. Here are some key recommendations from successful applicants to pass along to potential applicants:

- *Do not procrastinate on anything, ever. Read all of the requirements multiple times.*—**Rebecca Zaloudek, 2010 fellow (TN)** *(BA and MA from the University of Memphis)*
- *Timing is key, I know of many prospective fellows who didn't hear about the scholarship until they were ineligible to apply or until the application deadline had passed. I think I applied before I was officially accepted to Columbia, but a lot of students don't start looking for fellowships until after they are accepted.*—**Madison Kantzer, 2013 fellow (MD)** *(BA from Penn State University and MA from Teachers' College at Columbia)*
- *Ponder what a Madison Fellowship means for your life's work, and take notes on your thoughts and observations about history, especially U.S. constitutional history, to which you can refer when writing your application essays. Keep in touch with your best mentors in the education and history departments for both their counsel and their letters of reference.*—**Amanda Read, 2016 fellow (AL)** *(BA from Troy University and studying at Jacksonville State)*

In 1822, James Madison commented, "What spectacle can be more edifying or more seasonable, than that of Liberty and Learning, each leaning on the other for their mutual and surest support?" In 2017, Benjamin

Gies, a 2014 fellow from Kentucky with a BA from Bellarmine and an MA from University of Louisville, reports, "I currently teach U.S. History, serve as Vice President of the Kentucky Council for the Social Studies, and was recently elected as the youngest citizen to ever serve on our County Board of Education. More than anything else in my career, the James Madison Memorial Fellowship has given me these remarkable opportunities. I have been able to indulge in my passion for both history and for education." Mr. Madison would be proud!

## Note

1. For additional information and detailed regulations about the foundation and the fellowship program, or to open and complete an online application, please visit the foundation's website, www.jamesmadison.gov or email madison@scholarshipamerica.org.

# 4

# Suspenders and a Belt
## Overpreparation and the Overachiever

## TARA YGLESIAS

*Tara Yglesias* has served as the deputy executive secretary of the Truman
Foundation for the past thirteen years and has been involved in the selection
of Truman Scholars since 2001. During this time, she had the opportunity to
study the trends and characteristics of each incoming class of scholars. She
used this knowledge to assist in the development of new foundation programs
and initiatives as well as the design of two new foundation websites and
online application systems. An attorney by training, she began her career in
the Office of the Public Defender in Fulton County, Georgia. She specialized
in trial work and serious felonies but also assisted with the training of new
attorneys. A former Truman Scholar from Pennsylvania, she also served as a
Senior Scholar at Truman Scholars Leadership Week and the foundation's
Public Service Law Conference prior to joining the foundation's staff.

Little is more prized among the Truman community than the privilege
of sitting on a Regional Review Panel. These are the panels that select
our scholars and thereby identify tomorrow's public service leaders. These
spots are jealously guarded and turnover is infrequent. We have several
panelists whose service began in the 1990s. Both Dr. Andy Rich (chapter 1
in this volume) and I have served on Truman panels since the early 2000s.
So those of us who participate in Truman interview panels tend to take
the long view of history.

We will see short trend cycles. Who does not remember when tuber-
culosis had a moment circa 2004[1] or that time jumpsuits made a mild
interview fashion splash in 2015?[2] But major shifts in applications or applicants take years to emerge. Yet in 2016, we reached a sudden tipping
point on a trend that had been building ever since the first hand-wringing
think piece on millennials hit the pages of *The Chronicle*. Our candidates
were overprepared.

We have seen candidates suffering from this malady before—canned
responses have been the bane of the interviewer's existence at least since
someone coined the phrase "talking points," but 2016 was unusual. Early
in the cycle, we started hearing feedback like:

- *It is as if they are accessing files of information and reading them to me.*
- *I wish they had abandoned their talking points and interacted with the panel more.*
- *They seemed unwilling to engage with the questions.*

The interviews had a bit of a surreal quality to them—we would ask
questions that seemed to register only slightly with the candidate and yet
the candidate produced a comprehensive answer. But these interviews felt
like shaking a very wordy Magic 8 Ball. The answers, while comprehensive, were often not responsive. Generally, the feedback from our interview panelists is unbridled enthusiasm mixed in with pleas to allow them
to award more scholarships. This year was different.

After one early panel, we had a long discussion and came to the conclusion that part of the problem was that these students were lacking in
authenticity. But it was not that they never had authenticity—it was that
the authenticity had been wrung from them. After hearing one candidate
describe a series of "murder boards" that seemed more vigorous than most

dissertation defenses, and having no other candidate find this description at all strange, we settled upon the word "overprepared" as a fine catch-all to describe what we were seeing. This word seems to encapsulate all the problems—lack of engagement, inability to stretch intellectually, lack of displayed passion or authenticity—but it also acknowledged that students were taking this seriously.

We were still selecting the same scholars that we would have otherwise—and not every student who came before us could be categorized as overprepared. But for a good portion, if not an outright majority, their earnest preparation now threatened to be their undoing. We noticed this issue across gender presentation, institution, and geography. Preparation is intended to make the interview experience better, but for the overprepared student, the opportunity to test their mettle was likely unsatisfying. Once students have had eleven practice interviews, they really have seen it all. But in an effort to improve things for those who remained to be interviewed, I dashed off an email to the NAFA listserv, started warning candidates not to be too reliant on practice sessions, and we rode out the rest of the cycle.

But then overprepared began to have a moment.

## How Is It Possible to Overprepare?

After this year's presidential debates, MSNBC's Chuck Todd criticized Hillary Clinton for being overprepared.[3] Discussions unfolded about whether it is even possible to overprepare and, assuming it is, whether overpreparedness is worthy of criticism. Attempts were made to justify and explain the term as a substitute for everything from clarity of expression to authenticity of delivery. The concept of overprepared as a criticism was derided as a gendered insult—a way to communicate that a woman was demonstrating unseemly ambition or was being more intellectual than acceptable.

Which left me with our earlier assessment of our overprepared Truman candidates and how strange it was to be talking about students being too prepared. Were we criticizing them for taking this too seriously? Are we using "overprepared" as a code word for something else? Had a scholarship that often rewards the wonky just turned on the wonks?

Absent perhaps assuming leadership of an entire country, most human endeavor has a point at which preparation has diminishing returns. Studying into the wee hours versus getting a decent night's sleep, for instance. At some point after diminishing returns, preparation begins to turn on the diligent. That is when, for example, the overplanned family vacation turns into a bleak hellscape.[4]

But in these instances neither the diligent student nor National Lampoon's Clark Griswold can be fairly criticized for overpreparing—and the same is true of Truman candidates. These students are taking the process seriously and investing time and effort into being successful. Taking the process seriously is not worthy of criticism, but it is subject to critique.

## Sounds Like Someone's Got a Case of the "Overs"

Our critique began with looking at our panels and honestly evaluating the feedback we were getting to see if we were using "overprepared" as a code word for something else. Our first concern, in light of the criticism swirling around the word as a gendered insult, was to see to whom this term applied.

Overpreparedness was ecumenical in a lot of ways: we received feedback from every panel; the issue was not specific to particular schools;[5] and a representative number of students across gender presentations was affected. There was some variation in how overpreparation manifested itself. Some candidates were anxious, others glib. We saw those with polished scripts and those unable to utter complete sentences. There were interviews where candidates seemed wholly inauthentic, and then others where candidates were so agitated that their entire psyche appeared on display. Even with this constellation of symptoms, the panelists were certain that overpreparation was the culprit because all of these candidates had a few things in common:

- *They were overscripted*: All candidates should have a certain set of points that they wish to cover during the interview. It is acceptable to consider responses to frequently asked interview questions. But there is a point after which we descend into madness. No matter the nuance of the question, the candidate is going to shoehorn in that response everyone on Practice Interview #12 enjoyed so much. Instead of a flowing conversation, the interview feels as if the candidate is trying to recite a long-form poem but keeps getting interrupted with unrelated questions.[6] Candidates may artfully arrange not only their responses, but also their "casual" interactions with the panel.[7] Occasionally, we come across a candidate who has scripted their entire persona, focusing on the Truman not out of a genuine interest in public service, but out of an attempt to seek accolades. Both the robotic know-it-all (entirely scripted answers) and the odious toady (entirely scripted persona) were criticized by our panelists for a lack of authenticity. This lack of authenticity leads to an unsatisfying interview for all concerned.

- *They are overwrought*: Nerves are perfectly normal and should vary by candidate. But over the past several years, candidates have become increasingly overwrought at all aspects of the interview process. What used to be a charming amount of second guessing about their answers has morphed into a postmortem that is simultaneous with the interview itself. We are seeing more candidates who freeze during the interview or burst into tears during or immediately after. We often see them slumped on a cell phone in the hallway vividly re-creating the interview for their trusted confidant with purple prose and dizzying inaccuracy. The overwrought candidate may take every question as a personal affront, unable to engage in the sort of intellectual exercise that is a necessary part of a thorough interview. Others carry the burdens of the hopes of others into the interview; while these burdens can be helpful and informative of a candidate's motivations, such pressure can also be the undoing of a candidate.

- *They are overwhelmed*: Interviews are complicated and mystical things, so it is only natural for candidates to feel a bit overwhelmed. Candidates are presented with a huge volume of information—from our website, from their school, from former Truman Scholars—and have no understanding of how to synthesize any of it. I have promised myself not to engage in millennial bashing, but this generation of candidates is both unused to failure and more anxious overall.[8] These are the candidates for whom practice interviews ratchet up stress levels because that experience suggests to them that there is a "right" answer if they just look hard enough. After every question, interviewers watch as they try to synthesize various contradictory bits of feedback into a unified whole—thus they will be authentic and measured, passionate and pragmatic, chatty and formal all at the same time. The overwhelmed candidate can have the least satisfying experience of all. Often they spend more effort on the Sisyphean task of figuring out the "right" answer than allowing the panel to get to know them.

## You Promised No Millennial Bashing, but . . .

Overprepared students are nothing new to the world of competitive scholarships. On some level, our stock in trade is the kid who always has time to make another set of flashcards, read another article, and set up another informational interview. But we have quickly gone from the charmingly wonky candidate who tries to insert a Harry Truman reference just to show he made it through David McCullough's doorstop of a biography, to hordes of simulacra of this candidate, entirely without the charm. But the interesting part is that the candidates we are seeing have the charm and personality needed to have a good interview experience, but they cannot manage to show us what their recommendation writers see.

In many ways, millennials are uniquely prone to the downsides of overpreparation. First, millennials report more stress than any other generation.[9] They are naturally going to fall into the "overwhelmed" category and stay there. Additionally, these students are ill-equipped to deal with stress.[10] We cannot expect students to enter the interview stress-free. Indeed, my recollection of my own blasé generation X–style interview suggests that we do not want to return to the dystopian past either. But candidates need to be able to manage their stress levels in the lead up to the interview so that they can engage the panel without resorting to either dry recitation or unhinged spectacle.

Second, millennials tend to function more collaboratively than previous generations. We see the change in their applications. Gone are the days of campus dictators; we are in the era of leadership councils and copresidents. Setting aside the issues that this collaboration presents when trying to suss out whether a candidate is a leader and change agent, the collaboration leads to the unintended consequence of creating a stress echo chamber. Everyone on leadership council is invested in the candidate, and they are all stressed out. Well-meaning friends and mentors try to help in ways that only exacerbate the problem. Then the pressure to keep up with friends ("She did seven practice interviews, and I have only done six!") can undo any effort at moderation and appropriate preparation.

Finally, and speaking of keeping up with friends, the Internet certainly plays a role in the overpreparation of these students. In the dark ages, pre–dial-up candidates were limited in the information to which they had access. Schools could provide contacts and advice, there were probably some physical books at the library, and the truly ambitious would find an actual phone book and reach out to past candidates and recipients of an award. But today, candidates are able to reach out to any past candidate or recipient through a click of a mouse. While this development is generally positive and has opened the competition to candidates from a wide array of institutions, such ease of access also complicates things. Candidates begin to compare themselves—favorably or not—to profiles they read on the Internet. They reach out to candidates and winners, taking their advice, no matter how contradictory or inapplicable, and try to apply it to their own candidacy. When they have exhausted those routes, candidates venture down the dark path of random googling, finding all manner of inaccurate advice and attempting to synthesize it with all the other pieces of advice that they have received. Then candidates reflexively check in on social media to see how many of their friends had practice interviews that day. These tendencies result in a toxic slurry that can undo any candidate not able to properly evaluate the advice they are receiving.

## I've Unplugged the Internet; What Else Should I Do?

At the outset, we should recognize that the best Truman candidates are the overachievers, and there is almost nothing one can do to stop an overachiever from attempting to overachieve. These candidates will, regardless of instruction, worry and do and think too much about their interview. If these candidates are using preparation as armor, the goal of the advisor is to keep them from adding so much protection that they can never walk into battle.

Advisors should begin by having an honest conversation about the level of preparation they recommend. This comment assumes that the advisor has begun to *really* think about this question as well. It is imperative that advisors spend some time thinking about the value of different types of preparation. We recognize that some of these items are outside of the advisor's control. Some will likely not get away with giving one student four practice sessions and another two, even if that makes the most sense for the candidate. But advisors can make the practice sessions more or less formal, depending on the candidate. Consider what is driving certain exercises. Will they be beneficial for the student? Or are they practices that should be abandoned?[11]

After reviewing both the foundation's and the student's materials,[12] the advisor should have a frank discussion with the candidate about the type of preparation that is recommended and the type that is not. This information should be moderated depending on the candidate. But at a minimum, candidates need to be told how to sift through the advice they are receiving. Not all well-meaning advice needs to be followed. People tend to give advice from their own personal interests and shortcomings, so candidates should keep that in mind when deciding which information to rely upon. While our process changes little from year to year, current information is generally more reliable than even the most persuasive alumnus Truman Scholar. And, above all, keep in mind that we have never told anyone why they were selected.[13] Beware of anyone claiming to have the answer to the question of how one gets selected to be a Truman Scholar.

Which brings me to the most sensitive topic for any NAFA member: the answers and who has them. Some questions have answers (what are your stated criteria?) and others do not (how do those criteria get applied over a variety of factors that we cannot possibly know or control for?). How much preparation is needed to become a Truman Scholar is one of those questions without an answer. Or, to be fair, without an answer that either the foundation or advisors would want to share with people. Because there is no amount of preparation that will make someone a Truman Scholar. There is the amount of preparation needed to allow candidates to be authentic and as comfortable as possible, but that only allows them to have a valuable interview experience; it does not guarantee success.

But if we focus on the value of the process, we can offer all candidates a valuable and useful experience. After providing sound and persuasive advice about the need to stay off Google and the inappropriateness of canned response flashcards, advisors will find that candidates will do these things anyway. Most candidates are able to recite all the questions they were asked in their practice interview.[14] All of them. The only result of such an exercise is that they can then answer any question—but only the way it was posed to them during their mock interview. At that point, advisors need to shake up the process in order to get any positive results. One way to do that is by altering the type of questions asked during practice interviews. Committee members need to take specific policy positions they might not otherwise take and argue from those positions. Advisors should bring in real-world practitioners to ask questions from procedural and grassroots perspectives as well as questions outside the candidate's field.[15] Even something as simple as moving to a different location for an interview or asking the candidate to wear a suit can help them to engage rather than go on performance autopilot.

Affirmatively encourage candidates to stay out of the dark corners of the Internet. If they must google, have them google news articles related to their topic of interest. It is of course possible for that to go wrong as well, but then we are back into charming wonk territory and that is fine with us. Tell them to be judicious about who they reach out to for advice and how to apply it to their own situations. Remind them of the uniqueness of the interview process—what worked for one person in one situation is not likely to work again, simply because that interview will never be conducted the same way twice.

Each application and each applicant is distinct—the point of the interview is to try to understand those distinctions and see how well they match up with the goals of our program. For us, a successful process is one in which we are able to find those candidates who best match our goals, while providing a valuable experience for those candidates who are not selected. Candidates who present themselves authentically, even if that means they are less than perfect, stand a much better chance of not only being selected as a Truman Scholar, but also finding the process valuable when they are not selected. Advisors should encourage candidates to underprepare a bit—just this once—to have a much more worthwhile interview experience.

## Notes

1. TB's moment in the Truman application sun coincided with the publication of Tracy Kidder's *Mountains Beyond Mountains*, a book focused on Dr. Paul Farmer's efforts to fight TB in Haiti.

2. Net-a-Porter added "jumpsuits" as a category in 2014.

3. Danielle Paquette, "What We Mean When We Say Hillary Clinton Overprepared for the Debate," *The Washington Post*, September 27, 2016.

4. See, e.g., *National Lampoon's Vacation* (1983).

5. But we did notice that the problem of being overprepared was more frequent at schools that were also NAFA members. This tendency is likely a function of NAFA schools being generally more invested in preparation. (Regardless, it was interesting to note. All the good stuff is always in the footnotes.)

6. I like to imagine it is *Rime of the Ancient Mariner*.

7. The overuse of "That is a great question, Dr. X" is a fine example of this behavior.

8. Caroline Beaton, "Why Millennials Are So Stressed and What to Do about It," *Psychology Today*, September 5, 2015.

9. Ibid.

10. Taylor Clark, "It's Not the Job Market," *Slate*, January 31, 2011.

11. Again, we are sensitive to the pressure that some offices have placed upon them to produce deliverables, either in terms of materials or interviews. But while advisors may have others dictating the workload, they can exert some control over the level of stress the material places on their students.

12. Fear not, the Truman Foundation did not escape the audit either. We reviewed our written materials over the summer and left most intact. In our case, we are striking a balance between providing too much information to students who must already sift through a ton of material and being the sole provider for those students without strong advisors. We will also be reaching out to our alumni community on this issue. They often provide assistance and could help us in this endeavor.

13. I would be remiss to not make one of my favorite points here: It is extremely rare that someone is made a Truman Scholar because of one discrete thing. We select based on a totality of circumstances and often rely on impressions that are difficult to communicate outside of the interview selection room.

14. Candidates also seem to believe it is appropriate to tell our panel how we stacked up compared to their practice sessions. A general "this interview was not as bad as my practices" is fine, if ill-advised, but providing the interview panel with an assessment of how their questions rate compared to the ones from campus interviews just encourages a panelist to try even harder to stump the candidate.

15. Most of our panelists are not academics.

# Part II

## Serving Students

# 5

# Student Engagement
## A Road to Travel More

## KARNA WALTER

---

*Karna Walter is assistant dean for student engagement in the Honors College at the University of Arizona. The Office of Nationally Competitive Scholarships, housed in Honors, reports directly to her. A 1993 graduate of Calvin College, she earned a PhD in Higher Education at the University of Arizona. Walter oversees student engagement efforts in Honors, developing opportunities for students in research, civic engagement, study abroad, and internships. She leads Honors orientation programming and also the First-Year Experience for Honors students; both afford opportunities for connection with top students on the cusp of undergraduate life. She teaches Honors seminars regularly on human trafficking. Walter has also served on multiple review committees for nationally competitive awards.*

---

What is the purpose of higher education in the United States?[1] A simple question with a simple answer, right? No, actually. Ask a cross section of fellow Americans and responses will vary greatly. I posed this question to a diverse group that included current high school and college students. Those responding represent a wide spectrum of life experiences and characteristics, and their answers reflected some of this range. Although the seventy responses I received covered a wide spectrum, they fell into several categories: to contribute to my society and the world; to be successful in my career and life; to do better than my parents did economically; and to develop critical thinking skills necessary for being a leader.

One's perspective on this question is likely shaped by a variety of personal and social factors. A first-generation college freshman from a working-class family may have a very different view of higher education than a college student with a long-standing family legacy of college attendance. A university president might have a particular understanding of the aims of her university, one very different from a member of the community in which the university is situated. An employer looking for college graduates to fill open positions may have a different expectation for what higher education provides than a scholarship reviewer for a nationally competitive scholarship. Despite different impressions about the purpose of higher education, most people agree that a college education in some way advances an individual student's prospects in life (private benefits), and also, in a democracy, adds value to the civic fabric of a community, a state, and a country (public benefits).

The question about the aim of higher education is the subject of serious inquiry among educational researchers, university administrators, government officials, and others with a stake in the answer. The question begets more questions. If higher education is, at least in part, about educating undergraduates, then is a college education primarily about the individual student, what he stands to gain professionally and economically from earning a college degree? Is it about ensuring that the student acquires new knowledge? That she is prepared to enter the global economy? Is a college education about strengthening the common good, graduating students who put their education to use in solving societal problems? Is it all of the above? Colleges and universities are increasingly asked to do it all—to prepare students for entry into the global economy while also containing the costs of attendance and promoting access and completion. These same institutions are expected to educate students for lives of public service as well.[2]

If we accept that colleges and universities bear responsibility for addressing multiple purposes—helping individuals reach their potential and become prepared for life after college, while also ensuring that our students and graduates contribute to the public good—then scholarship advisors have a frame for the work they do on campus. Most individual institutions are creating structures that promote these purposes, which have implications for the educational practices and programs advisors develop.

## The Value of Student Engagement for the Work of Scholarship Professionals

Why should scholarship advisors care about these multiple purposes? An informal discussion with scholarship professionals shows that they are an altruistic lot. Most genuinely care for students and believe in them. Advisors typically want their students to reach their own potential—possibly even to win scholarships—but even more than that, advisors want students to harness their talents in the most meaningful ways possible, ideally using those talents to advance the common good through research, service, entrepreneurship, creativity, leadership, or a host of other areas.

But do our students arrive on our campuses fully formed, having done all it is they can or will do to become the people they are meant to be? Likely not. So college is a critical time of growth, change, and exposure to new experiences that will shape their personal and professional trajectories. Some of them are highly self-directed and will make their own opportunities, though such students are the exception to the rule. Most—arguably all—students will benefit from a campus culture that promotes student engagement. This student engagement will stretch students beyond the bounds of knowledge acquisition, asking them to apply what they are learning in new ways, in new contexts. Engagement allows them to develop knowledge and skills that they do not possess already. Institutions ask students to reflect on what they are learning and doing, making changes to their thinking and activity in ways that mature them, deepen them, and make them ready for the challenges they will face prior to and after graduation. Some, with a clearer sense of direction and purpose, will be ready and well positioned to apply for nationally competitive scholarships.

## Student Engagement

A movement toward student engagement is a recent trend on college and university campuses. Student engagement, at its best, addresses the dual challenge of offering personal and public benefits to our students, graduates, and communities. So what is student engagement, really?

The term *student engagement* may have different names on different campuses, such as experiential learning or education, service learning, engaged learning, or civic learning. Grounded in John Dewey's educational philosophy,[3] student engagement refers to the opportunity for students to apply what they learn in the classroom to new settings and contexts, effectively participating in the educational experience rather than being passive recipients of knowledge. Student engagement can happen as part of an existing, credit-bearing course or in university-curated experiences that might not be credit-bearing but that offer guided intellectual and practical value nonetheless.

At the University of Arizona (UA), the term *student engagement* refers to the promotion of engaged or experiential learning opportunities for every student on campus. These experiences include civic engagement, research, study abroad, internships, leadership experiences, and the like. Students may select from a range of credit-bearing and non-credit-bearing experiences that earn them an "engaged scholar" notation on the transcript. These experiences are vetted carefully by a multifaceted campus committee that screens them on a variety of levels, including intellectual and theoretical rigor, quality of experience, and opportunity for student reflection.

The Office of Student Engagement at UA has rolled out the 100 Percent Engagement Initiative over the past few years and is steadily building institutional knowledge and infrastructure to support the initiative. Although students are not required to complete an engaged learning experience, UA has built incentives, including a transcript notation, for those who do. Certainly, many of our students and faculty were involved in student engagement long before the initiative was implemented. Yet the office has elevated campus understanding about what student engagement actually is, offering incentives to faculty and staff who are facilitating student engagement experiences already to continue, and encouraging other faculty and staff to consider developing new student engagement proposals for existing or new classes, or for noncredit experiences that are benefi-cial to students and to other constituents. Such experiences are the fertile ground on which prospective scholarship applicants do the rigorous, in-depth, meaningful work that often becomes the basis for applications for a whole host of awards. Before considering what scholarship professionals can do to advocate for student engagement on campus, it is useful to take a closer look at the venues in which student engagement happens, and the aims of the best engaged learning experiences.

## High-Impact Educational Practices

So what kinds of experiences enable the deep involvement described pre-viously? How do college and university faculty and staff create these rich opportunities across different parts of the campus community? One im-portant point to reiterate is that engagement can happen in credit-bearing experiences and also non-credit-bearing experiences. Whatever the con-text, these opportunities enable students to do the kind of application of knowledge and reflection necessary to strengthen their own skills while also making a positive difference. These experiences also contribute to student retention, an important metric for college and university admin-istrators and (of course) a very important metric for students themselves who remain in college to earn a degree.

George Kuh promotes a series of teaching and learning practices that have been widely tested and have been shown to be beneficial for college students from a variety of backgrounds.[4] These practices have a positive impact on student retention and student engagement, thereby offering a strong foundation for students to build upon when developing plans for the future, both for their own benefit and for the common good.[5] Among these practices are:

- *First-Year Seminars and Experiences*: Courses for small groups of first-year students to engage with each other and with faculty on a regular basis.
- *Common Intellectual Experiences*: The modern version of the "core" curriculum that offers a set of requirements and/or shared experi-ences expected of all students.
- *Learning Communities*: Integration of learning across courses, with

students sharing two or more courses in common, working closely with the faculty.

- *Writing-Intensive Courses*: Writing expected at all levels of instruction and across the curriculum.
- *Collaborative Assignments and Projects*: Learning to solve problems and tackle challenges with other people, including those who may offer different experiences and perspectives.
- *Undergraduate Research*: Research experiences for students in all disciplines, tackling actively contested questions or creative challenges from the point of view of a researcher seeking new knowledge.
- *Diversity/Global Learning*: Curricular opportunities to learn about cultures, life experiences, and worldviews different from one's own; a prominent feature is study abroad.
- *Service Learning, Community-Based Learning*: Field-based experiential learning in a variety of contexts; requires application of learning and reflection.
- *Internships*: Direct experience in a work setting that involves oversight and coaching from professionals in the field.
- *Capstone Courses and Projects*: Culminating experiences that require graduating students to synthesize and apply what they have learned.

Some of these practices are embedded in the curriculum, with colleges and universities offering different levels of commitment and support for their value. Some are built into the co-curricular landscape and may or may not come with credit attached. Again, colleges and universities provide varying levels of structural support and incentives for faculty and staff to embrace these engaged learning practices and to encourage their students to engage in these ways. Scholarship professionals should take a close look to see where student engagement is happening on campus, whether there are offices whose mission is to promote and facilitate engaged learning (i.e., a center for civic engagement or a unit that promotes excellence in teaching), and if there are less obvious places where engaged learning is done well, such as an academic department that offers uniquely engaging internship opportunities, or a faculty member who has a reputation for deep engagement within his courses. The students who participate meaningfully in these experiences have the potential to be excellent candidates for nationally competitive scholarships because of both the substance of the experiences and the deep reflection about their work.

Scholarship professionals who know the landscape for engagement on campus will be able to cultivate relationships with the faculty and staff who are most important to identifying strong candidates for awards. For example, one tactic is to ask faculty in first-year seminars to nominate strong first-year students as potential applicants. Another is to work with staff involved in leading undergraduate research initiatives on campus to see which students stand out as having potential for research-specific awards. Yet another idea is to speak with staff and faculty engaged with study abroad, service learning, and internships, asking them to identify undergraduates who are most articulate about their experiences and have substantive leadership or initiative to discuss. Scholarship professionals cannot know every single student who could be competitive for awards even on the smallest of campuses. Knowing where robust engagement is happening and forging connections with the faculty and staff in direct contact with top students will yield a pipeline to the students most appropriate for outreach at different points in the life cycle of the student.

## Guiding Principles for Student Engagement

Developing the structures for student engagement on campus does not mean engaged learning is actually happening. Advocates must assess whether students are truly engaging in ways that are beneficial to them as developing students and also as societal contributors. The National Society for Experiential Education (NSEE) offers Eight Principles of Good Practice for All Experiential Learning Activities to serve as a guide for both the student participant and the faculty member or learning facilitator.[6] The Eight Principles include intention; preparedness; authenticity; *reflection* (my emphasis); orientation and training; monitoring and continuous improvement; assessment and evaluation; and acknowledgment. These principles help turn an experience into a highly valuable learning opportunity, if the student and learning facilitator optimize the experience rather than just "showing up" and putting in the time. One particularly noteworthy principle that is especially useful for prospective scholarship applicants is NSEE's principle of reflection:

*Reflection is the element that transforms simple experience to a learning experience. For knowledge to be discovered and internalized the learner must test assumptions and hypotheses about the outcomes of decisions and actions taken, then weigh the outcomes against past learning and future implications. This reflective process is integral to all phases of experiential learning, from identifying intention and choosing the experience, to considering preconceptions and observing how they change as the experience unfolds. Reflection is also an essential tool for adjusting the experience and measuring outcomes.[7]*

Reflection transforms the way a student interacts with an engaged learning experience. Reflection is not merely summative; it is also formative and allows students to have dynamic learning experiences. Exercising the "reflection" muscle is also a critical skill for students who may apply for scholarships. If students have not honed an ability to think critically about the needs of society and how they want to address them, why they are doing what they do, and how they can do it best, then they will have a harder time expressing their ideas in an interview, or writing persuasively about their aims for the future. They will also be less effective advocates for the issues important to them and for the areas in civic life that they will have a hand in changing. Reflection in undergraduate education is a means of strengthening individual students' growth while also contributing to the common good.

Reflecting on a previous example, the student who engages in a first-year seminar likely has many opportunities for reflection over the course of the seminar. Undertaking deliberative reflection from the first semester of college is an excellent habit to form for prospective scholarship applicants. Scholarship professionals who work with faculty to identify top students in the seminars, then offer more opportunities for students to engage in reflection at later moments (i.e., by inviting students to consider applying for awards and to complete a pre-application form), can help students leverage the range of their experiences toward competitiveness for awards.

## Advocating for Student Engagement Opportunities on Campus

If we agree that undergraduate education is about both private and public benefits, and that student engagement is an important pathway toward realizing those benefits, then what can scholarship professionals do to advocate for the most robust student engagement possible?

I offer several steps that may help reinforce an understanding of student engagement, assess what is available already on campus and in the community, and consider what advisors can do to support a culture of student engagement.

1. *Know the broader landscape for student engagement nationally.* Some advisors already have a good idea of what student engagement is and how it is done effectively. Others are less familiar with the term and have only a vague notion of what it means. Looking at national organizations as well as colleges and universities that have prioritized student engagement will give a better understanding of why this is an important topic and its value for scholarship applicants and the communities in which they are embedded. Organizations like Campus Compact, the National Society for Experiential Education, National Survey of Student Engagement, and the Association of American Colleges and Universities offer helpful research.

2. *Know the campus.* Take a good look at what is available formally (i.e., through the structures on campus, such as offices devoted to student engagement, or initiatives developed by university leaders, or career services offices) and informally (i.e., faculty or campus staff who are known for excellence in student engagement, as defined above). Have conversations with students, faculty, and staff about the concept of student engagement. Do people understand what it is and why it matters? Is there skepticism about the notion of "engaged learning" among certain groups, like faculty? Some faculty and staff may be involved in engaged learning without calling it that. Identify where the opportunities are to point students to experiences that offer robust student engagement. Cultivate strong relationships with the faculty and staff who will work with advisors to identify and encourage prospective applicants.

3. *Know the community and state.* What is the context in which the institution—and, therefore, its students—is imbedded? Are there ample, nearby opportunities for students to enter into? Is there a clear university process for students to engage in work with local nonprofits, do research with local companies, or get involved in local or state governance? Is there campus support for students to

earn credit for these opportunities? If students do work that will
not earn credit, is there some other designation that can indicate
the value of the experience? Be an advocate for students to deepen
their experiences while also earning recognition on campus for
what they do (i.e., a transcript designation or some special award).

4. *Offer opportunities for reflection to the students.* One of the most
valuable parts of student engagement is the opportunity for reflection on experiences. Students need to flex this muscle often and
well in order to become comfortable in communicating about
the things that matter to them. Even if students are not involved
in "official" student engagement experiences, advisors and faculty
members can offer them a valuable service by providing venues
for students to practice reflecting on the many and varied activities they participate in as undergraduates. Encouraging them to
do free writing exercises, or to create blogs, or to have small group
conversations with other students about their learning outside the
classroom will be invaluable.

## Undergraduate Student Engagement Matters

When considering the role institutions of higher education can play in
promoting student engagement as part of the landscape of undergraduate education, the Association of American Colleges and Universities offers a helpful perspective in "A Crucible Moment: College Learning and
Democracy's Future":

> *Americans still need to understand how their political system works and
> how to influence it. But they also need to understand the cultural and
> global contexts in which democracy is both deeply valued and deeply con-
> tested. Moreover, the competencies basic to democracy cannot be learned
> only by studying books; democratic knowledge and capabilities are honed
> through hands-on, face-to-face, active engagement in the midst of dif-
> fering perspectives about how to address the common problems that af-
> fect the wellbeing of the nation and the world. Civic learning that in-
> cludes knowledge, skills, values, and the capacity to work with others on
> civic and societal challenges can help increase the number of informed,
> thoughtful, and public-minded citizens well prepared to contribute in
> the context of the diverse, dynamic, globally connected United States. Civic*

*learning should prepare students with knowledge and for action in our communities.*

Regardless of how, where, and why students engage, they undoubtedly deepen their own preparation for a variety of pathways while also contributing to the common good. In the words of one who responded to my original question about the purpose of higher education, "I think an undergraduate education is both: it is about me and my growth, and it is also about how I can apply that growth to tackle the challenges, big and small, that we face in the world." By connecting often with offices that encourage, supervise, or coordinate student engagement, scholarship professionals, who have extensive networks on campus, can ensure that the students who have sought and embraced these meaningful experiences are also informed about scholarship opportunities. Nationally competitive awards can be the next step toward continued engagement and additional fulfillment of individual potential as well as the development of skills and connections that will help these students serve both private and public goals.

## Notes

1. The content of this chapter is drawn from a 2015 NAFA Conference presentation titled, "Trends in Higher Education: Contexts for Fellowship Advising." My thanks to fellow panelists Linda Dunleavy, Beth Fiori, Jonna Iocanno, and Paula Warrick for robust conversations around several themes, including student engagement. Thanks also goes to Abra McAndrew, assistant vice provost for student engagement at the University of Arizona, for expanding my understanding of student engagement on our campus.

2. Peter Levine, "A Defense of Higher Education and Its Civic Mission," *Journal of General Education* 73 (2014): 47–56; Jeff Selingo, *There Is Life after College: What Parents and Students Should Know about Navigating School to Prepare for Jobs Tomorrow* (New York: William Morrow, 2016); U.S. Department of Education, *A Test of Leadership Charting the Future of U.S. Higher Education: A Report of the Commission Appointed by Secretary of Education Margaret Spellings* (Washington, DC, 2006).

3. John Dewey, *Experience and Education* (New York: MacMillan and Company, 1938).

4. George D. Kuh, *High-Impact Educational Practices: What They Are, and Who Has Access to Them, and Why They Matter* (Washington, DC: Association of American Colleges and Universities, 2008).

5. The National Task Force on Civic Learning and Democratic Engagement, *A Crucible Moment: College Learning and Democracy's Future* (Washington, DC: Association of American Colleges and Universities, 2012).

6. Association of American Colleges and Universities, *Eight Principles of Good Practice for All Experiential Learning Activities* (Mt. Royal, NJ: National Society for Experiential Education, 2011).

7. Ibid.

# 6

# Scholarships as a Pathway to Government Service

## GIHAN FERNANDO

---

*Gihan Fernando is the executive director of the American University Career Center and has extensive experience in higher education administration with a focus on career services. Before joining the AU community, he held progressive leadership positions at the law schools at Georgetown University, Cornell University, and New York University. He has served as a reviewer for a $50 million United Negro College Fund grant program; a reader for the Truman Scholarship Foundation; and as a career consultant to the International Career Advancement Program (ICAP). He served as the president of the Board of Directors of NALP, the Association for Legal Career Professionals, from 2007 to 2008. Gihan is admitted to the District of Columbia and New York State bars, and before entering higher education practiced law at the McKenna & Cuneo law firm (now Dentons) in Washington, D.C. He is an honors graduate of Johns Hopkins University (BA, political economy) and received his JD degree from Georgetown University Law Center, where he was an associate editor on the* Georgetown

Law Journal. *Gihan grew up all over the world, primarily in Africa and Asia, and enjoys traveling to visit family and friends in Sri Lanka.*

---

**A**s executive director of the Career Center at American University (AU), one of the most interesting parts of my job is overseeing our Office of Merit Awards, under the leadership of Paula Warrick, a former NAFA president. When I joined American University in 2012, I already had twenty years of career services experience under my belt and was now working closely with scholarship and fellowships advising for the first time. The value of the connection between scholarship advising and career advising soon became clear to me. Many scholarship program applications have an explicit or implicit inquiry into what impact the candidate hopes to have on the world—which is another way of getting at the applicant's career aspirations and planning. Helping students to identify career goals and to articulate how the award will allow them to achieve their objectives is often an important part of a successful application.

I feel fortunate that there is a close structural connection between the Career Center and the Office of Merit Awards at AU. I know this is not common, and as a next-best alternative, I would advise the development of collaborative working relationships between scholarship advising and career services at any school where those do not already exist. I imagine that most career center colleagues would welcome scholarship advisors reaching out to them. Early in my time at AU, I was delighted to be included in a periodic happy hour where a few senior administrators from across campus would share a glass of wine, get to know each other on a more personal level, and better understand the common issues and challenges they face in their respective spheres. I am pleased to share some thoughts on the issues that scholarship advisors should consider as they meet with students who are interested in government service as their professional path. Knowing that there is a range of experience among NAFA members on career-related issues in general and government careers in particular, I have aimed my comments mainly at those who are less experienced in these issues. But I hope that certain sections, such as those on Presidential Management Fellowships (PMFs) and security clearances, may provide some useful background even for more experienced scholarship advisors.

## What Do Government Recruiters Look For?

That is a big question, to which there are many answers, but I will highlight here a few things to consider. As a general matter, most will want to see a commitment to public service, as demonstrated by a range of possible activities, such as volunteering, interning, service projects, and so on. In addition, many will want some demonstration of interest in the specific work of the government agency or department in which the student hopes to work. Coursework in that substantive area, relevant internships, and prior work experience in the field will all help a candidate be noticed. For example, students interested in joining the Department of State as a foreign service officer would benefit from having studied international relations, having a country or regional focus, experience of living and working abroad, and demonstrating a commitment to one of the specific areas within the State Department in which they are interested, such as public diplomacy, economics, consular affairs, or political matters.

## Creative Ways to Gain Government Experience

Most advisors are likely very familiar with state and local government opportunities in their regions, and perhaps more so than federal opportunities outside D.C. A frequent concern from students is whether working at the state and/or local level will limit their chances at the federal level. As a general matter, that is unlikely to be the case. Interning at the state or local level is a demonstration of a commitment to public service, and if the experience gained at the state or local level helps develop or demonstrate an interest area, that will likely be viewed positively by federal government recruiters at departments that work on similar issues.

In addition to the many state and local government opportunities around the country, think beyond the executive branch agencies. Many judges at all levels of government will gladly take interns, as will state legislators, or U.S. senators and representatives in their home state offices. Interning for a judge can provide valuable knowledge of many aspects of decision-making processes, develop writing and research skills, and hold out the possibility of a strong mentor relationship. Note that students can develop interests in certain issue areas for which there are specialized state or local courts, such as children's rights, family issues, and housing policy, by interning with a state or local court with a focused docket.

There are many federal offices that are located outside D.C., including many that focus on law enforcement (such as U.S. Attorneys' Offices); corrections (Bureau of Prisons, which falls under the Department of Justice); and national security (with many intelligence and security agencies having regional offices). Of course, many students can apply for summer internships with government offices in Washington, D.C. But internship opportunities, whether paid or unpaid, are most competitive in the summer, when students from around the country are all applying for such openings. If a school has a "Semester in Washington" program, it should make sure advisors are well acquainted with the program and help promote it to students. In addition, there are several programs in Washington that will accept students from any school, and which frequently include an internship component.

Some federal agencies are now starting to provide virtual internship programs. (Both the Department of Homeland Security and the State Department have well-developed programs.) While virtual internships will not provide the relationship-building and mentorship components of a live internship, there is value to the substantive experience that can be obtained through a virtual internship.

A frequent concern with government internships is the fact that so many of them are unpaid, limiting access to these valuable experiences to those who can afford to take them. I do not have an easy answer here beyond the ones that advisors likely already have thought about: some internships are paid, some schools will have funding programs to help support students in unpaid, career-building internships, and there are some scholarships that will provide support for study and/or internships.

## Help Students Develop a Substantive Area of Interest and Focus

This idea should be familiar to scholarship advisors, as it makes sense in most cases to identify the student's interest first and then consider which scholarship may support that interest, rather than the other way around. The same principle applies to a career in government: first identify the issue or substantive area in which the student wishes to focus and then work backward to identify scholarships that may provide funding for appropriate educational or experiential development to support that issue.

In addition to the usual tools that advisors use to help students identify a particular academic or issue focus (academic or personal interests, faculty mentors, conducting research and reading in an area), career services colleagues can help too. AU's career center routinely helps students, especially undergraduates, go through a process of self-reflection using tools such as the Myers-Briggs Type Indicator, the Strong Interest Inventory, and newer tools like Gallup's StrengthsFinder, to help identify substantive areas of work and workplace settings that fit well with the student's values and interests. In addition, career advisors can help students develop an effective campaign of informational interviews to confirm—or equally important, to reject—a particular issue or workplace setting as the area in which they hope to spend a significant part of their lives.

## Help the Student Think Broadly

Once the student has identified a focus that includes working in government as a possible pathway, help the student think broadly to uncover as many opportunities as possible. As noted above, there are many excellent federal opportunities beyond Washington, D.C., with state and local government. Even when focusing on federal service, a truism is that it is much easier to move around as an insider within the federal government system. So the first job may not be the exact one the student wanted, but it generally will be easier to move within and even across agencies and departments once an individual is within the federal system. Similarly, think beyond the obvious when it comes to working in a particular substantive area. Students interested in working on international issues may only think of the State Department, which may be the most competitive service to enter. Advisors may want to help students conduct research that uncovers less obvious international opportunities, such as the Department of Commerce for international trade and economic opportunities. It may surprise students to learn that the Department of Agriculture has large numbers of internationally focused economists and trade specialists who work on food accessibility and safety, trade, and nutrition-related matters. Similarly, students interested in national security should think beyond the CIA and the Department of Homeland Security, as there are at least seventeen independent intelligence services in the country.

## Pre-Graduation Scholarships

It is outside the scope of this essay to cover the weird and wonderful world of applying for a job with the federal government in any depth. Suffice it to say that students and advisors alike are well advised to conduct some in-depth research and seek information from knowledgeable sources such as the Partnership for Public Service, a nonprofit that seeks to inspire a new generation to serve in government. As with any job search, having performed well in an internship with a government office will give a student an advantage when applying for a permanent position with that office or a related agency (not to mention helping students develop a focus in a particular area of interest). Through internships, students gain valuable substantive experience, contacts, mentors, and knowledge of often opaque processes for accessing opportunities, thereby helping students obtain summer or semester internships, which can be an important part of their development and enhance their ability to access appropriate opportunities. Advising on scholarships that provide study and/or internship opportunities prior to graduation, such as PPIA, Udall, NOAA Hollings, and Killam, can likewise help students develop their substantive focus and make them stronger candidates for postgraduate scholarships as well as for government service.

In the remainder of this essay, I discuss scholarships by groupings as to how they may enrich and enhance a career in government service. It is impossible to be comprehensive here, so please view any highlighted scholarship programs as prominent examples and not as the entire universe of possibility. Inevitably, with changes happening in real time, some of this content will be out of date as of the writing, so consider this a broad guide that must be confirmed by further research.

## The Presidential Management Fellows Program

The Presidential Management Fellows Program (PMF) is the primary entry-level recruitment program for the federal government. It is structured as a two-year fellowship program intended to attract the best and brightest to government service, and upon successful completion, provides noncompetitive access to a career and leadership in government. The PMF program is open to those who will receive an advanced degree (e.g., master's, PhD, JD) or have received such a degree within the mandated period. The application process has multiple steps and has gone through several changes in recent years, so encourage candidates to seek advice from the PMF website for the relevant application year. In brief, as of this writing, the process is that eligible candidates complete an online assessment. If successful, they are named PMF finalists. Certain backgrounds, such as veterans or those in STEM fields, receive preferences. Being named a finalist makes the candidate eligible to interview with government agencies and departments that have slots open for PMF candidates. If successful in that interview process, the candidate is named a Presidential Management Fellow.

Universities handle advising for PMF in different ways, with the most common model being a disaggregated one where the career advising office in a particular graduate school takes responsibility for providing guidance to their interested students. A scholarship advisor should at minimum be aware of the broad parameters of how the program works and be able to refer interested students and graduates to appropriate on- and off-campus resources for further advising.

## Scholarship Programs That Provide a Pathway to Government Service

It goes without saying that highly selective scholarship programs like the Rhodes, Marshall, Gates, Schwarzman, and Truman will confer a level of prestige upon awardees and garner attention from any prospective employer, including many government employers. Outside of the select few who receive such an award in any given year, there are still many scholarship opportunities for those who wish to advance their public service career goals through a scholarship. As advisors know, many scholarships are set up to fund graduate study and research, with certain of these focusing in particular substantive areas. The Truman Scholarship is specifically intended to develop those interested in leadership in public service, and such graduates will find particular resonance with government departments that work on the issues in which the candidate developed knowledge through their graduate study and research. Others, like the Princeton in Latin America/Africa/Asia programs, provide the student with valuable overseas living and work experience, which is often hard to come by for a new graduate. Service as a Peace Corps volunteer is another structured program that can provide new graduates with the valuable experience of living and working in a foreign country for an extended period. Peace Corps recruitment and advising will likely come out of a career services office rather than through a scholarship advising office, so students who view the option of Peace Corps as a way to gain overseas experience may also find that it helps them get started with their research.

## Government Scholarships Intended to Develop U.S. Citizens

Fellowships advisors already know that many scholarship programs are funded by the federal government as a way of developing the skills and capabilities of the U.S. population. By virtue of that fact, nearly all such scholarships have a U.S. citizenship requirement of candidates. Scholarship programs such as Fulbright and Boren are examples of programs funded by the federal government with the goal of developing certain skills and abilities in U.S. citizenry. Fulbright awards of all kinds provide in-country experience and a people-to-people diplomacy component, and may include language acquisition or development. Fulbright research awards also help the individual develop a substantive focus through graduate study and research, while Fulbright English Teaching Awards provide language and teaching exposure. Boren Scholarships and Fellowships are specifically focused on developing language skills through immersive learning for an extended period in a country where the language is widely spoken and may include an internship component as well.

Many government agencies provide scholarships for research and study in the sciences. The National Science Foundation, NOAA Hollings, and Goldwater awards are but a few that immediately come to mind. As with Fulbright awards, these and others provide funding for study and research in a scientific field, and some include an internship in the relevant field. In addition, they confer prestige and some level of government vetting that will help the awardee in a search for a position with a government office after completion of the scholarship, as well as the intangible benefits of developing mentors and knowledge of processes for recruitment that can provide a significant advantage.

Certain government-funded scholarships are intended to attract high performing members of underrepresented groups to government service.

Usually, these scholarships provide both funding for study and a pathway to joining the agency funding the scholarship. Most prominent among such programs are those funded by the State Department, and include the Gilman (study abroad funding for students receiving Pell grants), the Rangel, and the Pickering (for students from underrepresented backgrounds). Both Rangel and Pickering provide two years of graduate study and mentoring and have a five-year service requirement. Both are pathways to a career with the Foreign Service. In addition to distinct application processes, another difference between Pickering and Rangel is that in the domestic internship/mentoring component, Pickering provides exposure to the State Department, while Rangel provides exposure to Capitol Hill.

These are but a few of the many opportunities available for students to develop work and research experience prior to and post graduation. Again, there are myriad scholarships available that can help position a student to acquire knowledge of and enhance their access to public service opportunities. Students will benefit from developing an area of interest and focus, and then conducting careful research, with appropriate guidance, into which scholarships will support their goals and dreams.

## A Word about Security Clearances

I would be remiss if I did not at least mention security clearances in an essay about government service. Many government agencies require a security clearance for prospective employees. What surprises many is that even internship opportunities may require some level of security clearance, depending on the subject matter, department, and location of the opportunity. There are several considerations to keep in mind:

> *Timeline*: Security clearances, even at the lowest level, can take four to six months to be approved, and the candidate cannot begin the internship or work assignment until the clearance comes through. Significant advance planning is therefore essential for opportunities that require a clearance. Even with advance planning, the timing can be out of the candidate's (and the agency's) control. For example, a student who has been offered a summer internship pending security clearance may not receive the clearance until August or later. Note that the government office that is recruiting cannot

usually influence the length of time it takes to obtain a clearance, a process that is normally handled by a completely separate government office.

*Preparing for the process*: As in life, it pays to be completely truthful in the clearance process. It is much better to reveal a possible issue candidly and fully than to have it come up unexpectedly in the course of a clearance investigation. It is helpful to gather all the information one will need, in particular, a list of addresses and contacts for the last many years. Ironically, extended overseas stays and contacts with non-U.S. citizens can lengthen the clearance process. Advise students who are traveling for summer, study abroad, or on scholarships to keep diligent records of where they lived and contact information for people with whom they interacted regularly. Students should also obtain a copy of their credit report and work through any issues on it.

*Issues that can delay a security clearance from being granted*: Illegal drug use (including use of marijuana in states and localities where it is legal) can be problematic. The general advice is to immediately stop use of any illegal substance, and the more time that has passed since the last use, the better. Also disclose all mental health issues and have records to demonstrate treatment plans, and so on. Only complete applications will be reviewed, which makes it particularly important to keep good records of the items requested on the clearance forms.

In closing, I strongly encourage scholarship advising and career services offices to partner and collaborate. As I write, the Trump administration is barely in office, and we have much uncertainty ahead, with a temporary federal government hiring freeze that may have an impact on scholarships with a service requirement. And funding for government scholarship programs may be affected as well. The changing times make it all the more important for all parts of the academy to collaborate with each other closely to enrich and encourage our students' aspirations to make change in the world through public service.

# 7

# Advising Students on the Many Roads of Study Abroad

## RICHARD MONTAUK

*Richard Montauk is the author of* How to Get into the Top Law Schools,
5th ed. *(Prentice Hall, 2011) and* How to Get into the Top MBA
Programs, 6th ed. *(Prentice Hall, 2012). He received a bachelor's degree
from Brown University, a master's in government from Harvard University,
and a master's in finance and a JD from Stanford University. Early in his
career he worked as a corporate lawyer for Latham & Watkins, then as a
corporate strategy consultant for Bain & Co. He was a recipient of a Rotary
Graduate International Ambassadorial Scholarship to study Common
Market law, as it was then known, at the London School of Economics and
Institute for Advanced Legal Analysis, London. He is a frequent presenter at
national and international conferences regarding law and business school
admission, as well as early career strategy. His forthcoming books include one
about advanced law degrees (LLMs) and another about "making real money"
during college, as well as a revised edition of* How to Get into the Top
Colleges.

**M**any students study abroad for one or more terms. Doing so offers exciting and rare opportunities to develop knowledge, skills, and self-understanding. This makes study abroad a highly appropriate focus for those who are seeking or who may seek a fellowship. This essay examines study abroad opportunities for undergraduates considering the possibility of going abroad for one or several terms. Much of this examination is also equally relevant to a graduate student considering studying abroad—or to someone applying for an international fellowship.

## Why Study Abroad

Students who study abroad do so for a variety of reasons. Among other things, they want to:

- develop foreign language skills or an in-depth, firsthand knowledge of a foreign culture.
- learn more about themselves, their family, or an aspect of their heritage (such as religion) and often hope to gain perspective on the world, including the United States. (Seeing how another culture operates makes it easier for students to understand what is unique about their own.)
- use study abroad to attend a top university and have the opportunity to meet people from around the world. Studying abroad can even allow some to pursue a subject not available at their college, and it allows all students from the United States to study a subject from a different perspective. Studying America's handling of the Cold War at an American campus is one thing; doing so in France (let alone Russia) provides a very different view.
- conduct research abroad, such as studying Sami culture in Finland. For most students, studying abroad opens doors to places that they have previously not visited.

Of course, some study abroad for entirely pragmatic reasons, such as to become more attractive to employers or graduate programs. Others do so because they believe they can develop their own abilities significantly. They may look to gain confidence by operating with less supervision and oversight. Studying abroad is also an opportunity to develop problem-solving, to learn to work independently, and to practice self-discipline. Most students return from a study abroad program with a greater sense of self and greater clarity of interests and values as well as a strong sense of responsibilities. Study abroad teaches a variety of skills including flexibility, adaptability, resilience, and reliability. All of these help students ready themselves for the next step, which often includes graduate schools and in some cases the desire to apply for nationally competitive scholarships in order to help them realize their increasingly clear postgraduate education and career paths.

## Transforming Students' Lives

Simply exposing students to a different culture would cause them to be transformed. This was thought to be particularly true for those students who were "immersed" in the experience. The evidence for this belief, however, was limited largely to students' self-reporting. Independent evaluations of their ability to live and work in a different society have been lacking.

More recent evaluations have demonstrated that many if not most students are little affected by their study abroad experience if they have pursued it in the traditional American fashion, which involves sending students abroad in the ultimate bubble: American students living with other American students, taught by American instructors, and encouraged to sightsee locally and travel regionally with a group of Americans. Any required language courses have been offered in the American fashion, too: the emphasis being on learning how to read and write the language, not to speak it—let alone to speak it as people do "in the street" (in real life, as opposed to the classroom). Mixing with locals—let alone meaningful engagement with the local culture—has been barely encouraged in some programs; most mixing only occurs with those who want to practice their English (or improve their skills at or knowledge of American sports).

Relatively few students are able to engage with the local culture on their own. To do so requires a large degree of confidence and nerve, as well as language skill. Well-designed programs recognize this and provide multiple means to overcome it. They are designed for longer stays abroad, taking classes with local students, living with host families, and joining in activities with locals. They discourage Americans teaming up with Americans for social activities, including travel.

Students learn a great deal more when their program involves substantial cultural mentoring, not just cultural immersion. For instance, some programs now require participation in a formal course, whether for academic credit or not, that pushes students to engage in various ways with the local culture. This might involve seeing films with locals, joining a university sports team, or working on an academic project with local students. On a weekly basis students participating in such experiences often write reflective comments, perhaps in response to set prompts, which describe their actions and reactions. These are posted for other students and the professor to discuss and give feedback.

Advisors guiding students through the process of choosing a study abroad program should favor one that is structured to help them integrate with locals, analyze and reflect on their learning, and so on. Most of these programs use the Intercultural Development Inventory to assess participants' learning. Advisors will also want to guide students toward the evaluation instrument the institution's program uses (if any). The following sections will help students choose programs that will maximize their learning.

## Choosing a Program

There are an intimidatingly large number of study abroad programs. The starting point is to help students assess their own needs and interests. Having a conversation about their education goals will help narrow the list of programs. Conversation topics should include:

- reasons for going abroad (academic enrichment, language learning, or connection with overseas family or family history).
- where they wish to study—a particular region, country, city.
- type of environment sought (capitol city, mountainous area, near particular flora or fauna).
- number of credits they need to earn.
- subjects they wish to study, including particular courses.
- whether they wish to be in an English language, foreign language, or mixed language academic environment.
- whether they want to live with other students (American, international, local) or a host family.
- the time they can afford to be away from their home university.

- the degree of structure they want in a program. Do they want their schedule in and out of class to be mandated, or do they want more freedom to determine what they will do?
- their extracurricular interests and needs (for example, a synagogue or mosque nearby).
- the amount they can afford to pay. Their eligibility for such need-based grants as Gilman or their desire to apply for a CLS or Boren Scholarship.

However, advisors may wish to discuss more personal issues as well, such as medical needs, sexual or gender identity issues, and family matters. Particular personal issues may require contact with specific programs or scholarship providers. It is better to fully understand the circumstances prior to going than have the students confront issues once they have arrived. All students are interested in the credit they will receive. Schools differ in their policies on this. Some will grant credit only for their own programs; or for those on a list of approved programs; or for those from any accredited American university; or for those from any recognized higher education organization in the world. Even schools that do not have a study abroad program or a procedure in place to grant credit may allow students to take a leave of absence for one or more terms so they can attend a program and then transfer credit back to the institution. Students need to be mindful that whatever the policies are, they will need to go through the required procedures to get approval. Scholarship advisors should be well versed in institutional policy because they will likely be seen as a first stop for assistance.

## Types of Programs

Study abroad programs can be usefully evaluated along two axes: (1) whether they are run by American universities or others, and (2) their degree of integration with local universities and the local community.

> *American Programs:* Many programs are run by American universities, but they are by no means all the same. Some are islands of Americanism in the midst of a foreign country; whereas, others make greater or lesser efforts to integrate students into foreign life. The programs are of three broad types:

1. *Island programs.* The students are American, and many or all professors are likely to be home-university faculty, with the remainder being hired directly by the home university. Courses may be taught in English or in the local language.
2. *Partially integrated programs.* These offer the opportunity to take courses at a foreign institution and at the American sponsoring institution. The courses at the American institution may be in the local language or in English. Courses at the foreign institution are likely to be more demanding, especially in terms of the language skills required.
3. *Integrated programs.* Students take classes at the local host university with local students. They may or may not have the opportunity to room with local students in local university dorms.

American programs—whichever of the three categories they are in—have some definite advantages. Application is generally easy. They often help with visa applications and other paperwork. They tend to make it easy to transfer credits and often provide prearranged housing, group trips, and possibly special language courses. Most programs, especially those that are of an island or semi-integrated nature, have full-time staff on site available to help.

*American non-university-sponsored programs*: Organizations such as the Council on International Educational Exchange sponsor many study abroad programs. These programs are generally similar to numbers 1 and 2 above insofar as they are designed for American students to take classes created specifically for them. Most of these programs are specifically for English-speaking students, so the opportunities to integrate with local students via classes are generally limited. Relatively few of these programs offer the opportunity to room in local university dormitories, further limiting the opportunity to integrate with local students. Individual colleges may have an agreement with the organization, which should make transferring credit easy for students. If students wish to sign up for such a program on their own, however, advisors should help them make sure that the college will accept their credits.

*Direct enrollment in a foreign university*: Some foreign universities permit students to enroll for a term or a year (classifying them as visiting or international students). American students take classes with regular students, taught by regular faculty, presumably in the local language. Students may be able to live in university housing. Application is generally through the foreign university's international student office.

This option is generally much less expensive than American options and is highly suited to mixing with locals. However, admission is likely to be time consuming and potentially awkward to arrange. Financial aid is unlikely to transfer (although the cheaper tuition may make this irrelevant). The student will probably have little support—only that from the foreign university's international student office and the home university's study abroad office, but not from on-the-ground personnel. Thus, the student will need strong language skills and a highly developed sense of independence. (The student should check with a suitable professor about his or her language skills.) In addition, students may face difficulty getting credit for courses, so students should be sure to arrange for it in advance.

## International Universities' Special Programs for Foreign Students

A number of universities have established new programs for non-native students. This is quite common in Europe, where universities have taken advantage of the Bologna Accords meant to standardize educational programs and credentials across the continent. The result has been universities creating programs designed for foreign students to come for a term or two (or for a full degree). These programs are usually taught in English.

Some programs allow students to enroll in the same courses as local students do. The London School of Economics (LSE), for example, offers the General Course, which is designed for students from around the world to attend courses on the same basis as regular LSE students. Registration for the course is simple and, because of its strong international reputation, many American colleges readily accept transfer credit from it.

## Key Differences between International and American Education

Many foreign universities teach much differently than American schools do. Much of American teaching is student-centered. Professors welcome student comments in class and out; make their expectations abundantly clear, with a detailed syllabus and painstaking descriptions of what to do in a paper or on an exam; and do not penalize for a failure to attend class or for playing on a digital device during class. In many other parts of the world, especially outside Anglophone and Northern European environments, teaching is more likely to be professor-centered and, as a result, may bear little resemblance to what American students take for granted. Even in England, which is relatively student-centered in orientation, they might be given a twenty-page list of readings and only a rudimentary syllabus, noting in a general way the topics to be covered each week. Students will be expected to read the articles and books that most interest them and contribute to class discussions on the basis of what they have read. The only grade may be a term-end or year-end final examination, which may consist of six questions, with students expected to answer two of them (chosen, presumably, on the basis of what they have read).

Most countries either make higher education free or subsidize it considerably, which means that students do not view themselves as paying customers entitled to highly personalized treatment. The trade-off is that they may have far more freedom to pursue aspects of a subject that interests them rather than hewing to a narrowly drawn syllabus.

Because study abroad programs that are open to students from different colleges want to attract customers, they visit American college campuses to promote their programs. These fairs occur throughout the year, but they are most common in the fall. Colleges that are big enough or send enough students abroad may be visited by such programs or they may visit a nearby school. In fact, many larger universities host a Study Abroad Fair that multiple programs attend. Program representatives set up a table or booth complete with brochures and course catalogues (and applications, of course). The representatives are happy to talk with interested students, so students planning to apply for Gilman, Fulbright, or Boren should definitely go to these fairs ready to engage with representatives.

## Timing Issue

Many American colleges permit study abroad only after students have completed most or all of their core requirements. Some also require that students have chosen a major and, perhaps, completed some courses in it.

As a result, most students will be unable to do a standard study abroad program before the second half of their sophomore year and possibly not until their junior year. (A substantial majority of those who study abroad do so during their junior year.)

Other important factors to consider are:

- whether a student plays a sport (and thus can go for only the less-active season).
- whether a student intends to write a senior-year thesis or undertake significant research.
- requirements for a student's major.
- whether the student is prepared to spend time away from their friends.

*Going abroad sophomore year*: If the student is eligible (having completed core or major courses, etc.), going abroad during their sophomore year has several advantages:

- Students can be back on their home campus for their junior and senior years, thereby making it easier to achieve school leadership positions, prepare for graduate study, and complete undergraduate research.
- They can push their language skills to a high level early in their college career, thereby opening up the opportunity to take advanced classes in it and even to work on another language.
- Earlier participants may be particularly attractive to employers for highly desired summer (and term-time) internships or for National Science Foundation Research Experiences for Undergraduates (NSF REUs) and other summer research programs, given their foreign achievements such as mastering a language, demonstrating drive, maturity, independence, and competence.
- These students can also get a jump on exploring a major or other academic focus insofar as the program allows. In-depth exposure to the field can help a student determine whether a field is the right fit, and even what aspect of it to explore further. It could even jump-start a senior thesis.
- Early participation can allow a student to go abroad more than

once and reap the benefits of experience in their second venture abroad.

Those who go abroad during the sophomore year usually do so during the spring semester because being ready to leave in the fall is nearly impossible even for the most organized of students.

Being ready to head abroad so early is not always easy. Even if the student has completed enough requirements to be allowed to go, chosen a major, finished any required language courses, and perhaps figured out her goals for studying abroad, she will still need to pick a program and make the necessary preparations to leave. And as this essay suggests, students should aim to get the maximum out of such a program, not just aim to do one.

*Going abroad junior year:* Junior year is the default year for study abroad. Nearly two-thirds of those who study abroad do so during their junior year, and many college programs limit study abroad to juniors. The advantage to studying abroad junior year is that the student can be completely ready to do so, having completed core courses, chosen a major, investigated study abroad options, and prepared thoroughly by taking multiple language courses, completing prerequisites for courses to be taken in the study abroad program, and so on. In addition, the student will be back on the home campus for the senior year, which allows direct access to professors and advisors and makes it easier to apply for graduate programs, jobs, and fellowships.

*Going abroad senior year:* Those who go abroad senior year generally do so because they have only lately figured out the great value of doing so. Others have only had the opportunity because of a change in circumstance, such as their thesis advisor or academic mentor doing a sabbatical abroad, or being injured and unable to compete in their sport (and thus able for the first time to travel abroad). Some go because they are planning a fifth year. There are several potential advantages to senior year study abroad. The student may have developed his language skills to a point that allows him to take foreign university classes with locals and to integrate relatively easily into life abroad. The student may know exactly what she wants to study and be in a position to explore a subject in depth because of her prior preparation during three years in college. The student may have exhausted the resources of the college in his chosen field and be able to access further resources in a foreign program.

The disadvantages, however, are several, too. Writing a thesis while abroad may be very difficult. It can also be difficult to apply for graduate programs or jobs (or fellowships) while abroad. The student may dislike being away from friends during the last year. These disadvantages can be minimized if a student limits the time abroad to just one semester and chooses the semester that will interfere least with graduate school and fellowship applications, for example.

*Going abroad during the summer*: Students may be unable to study abroad during the regular school year because of their athletic or other extracurricular commitments, or because their academic program is ill-suited to this. Engineering students, for instance, may find it nearly impossible to leave campus for a full semester. In that case, you might suggest that the student consider doing a summer abroad. However, many summer programs are different than those offered during the regular academic year:

- Some are mainly tours, with limited or no emphasis on academics, which may limit the student's ability to get school credit for them.
- Many are offered largely or exclusively for Americans and, with foreign universities often closed for the summer, the student may have little opportunity to interact with local students.
- Relatively few offer advanced science and engineering classes, choosing instead to emphasize arts, humanities, and social sciences.

In addition, students will probably have to forego the possibility of summer internships. Because summer internships are considered particularly valuable during the summer after junior year, you might guide students toward doing a summer study abroad earlier in their college career.

Scholarship advisors might also guide them toward exploring the various nationally competitive fellowships available for summer study abroad. These include the Fulbright UK Summer Institute, Fund for Education Abroad, Humanity in Action, Critical Language, Davis Projects for Peace, Boren, Freeman-Asia, Crimson Exchange, DAAD, and Laura Bush Traveling Fellowship (U.S. Department of State). Some colleges, especially the well-endowed ones, have summer grants for their own students.

*Taking advantage of intersession programs*: Many campuses are now offering study abroad opportunities associated with a course taught during an intersession (summer, winter, spring) with preparatory and follow-up work taking place on campus and then ten to fourteen days being spent abroad. This is the briefest of study abroad experiences with the advantages and disadvantages that go along with brevity. These experiences can be exhilarating, create a team-building atmosphere, and provide a broader view of the subject matter for the course, but they should not be seen as the ideal study abroad experience as students simply do not have time to understand the culture or develop language skills. Again for some fields like engineering or business, this may be, however, a student's only opportunity before pursuing graduate study especially if the student's summers are filled with research programs, internships, or co-op experiences. If a student is planning to apply for a graduate program abroad (and for awards like Rhodes, Marshall, Gates Cambridge, Fulbright, etc.), then even a short experience like this will say to a selection committee that the student is willing to embrace another culture, can adjust to the demands of travel, and wants to understand another perspective.

One final note regarding timing. The simple rule of thumb is, the longer, the better. Encourage students to consider going abroad for a full year, because this length of time:

- offers substantial opportunity to become truly fluent in another language—and to integrate into the community;
- makes it much easier to make friends with local students and other locals;
- offers the opportunity to become fully knowledgeable about the city and culture;
- fits better with some university systems, such as those in the UK, which offer most courses on a full-year basis and thereby limit eligibility to students who plan on staying a full academic year; and
- allows the possibility of studying in two different locations, perhaps in two different languages.

## Funding the Trip

Students will likely have questions about how to fund their experiences abroad. The school's study abroad and financial aid offices may be best suited to answer such questions specifically; however, here are a few general guidelines.

*Financial Aid:* If students head abroad on a program sponsored by the home university, financial aid (other than federal work study) will probably transfer. Students are likely to pay approximately the same amount for time abroad (except for transportation to and from) that they would pay for continuing to study at the home campus. The same is true if students travel abroad through programs that other American universities sponsor, assuming that home universities have agreements with them.

If the student enrolls directly at a foreign university, he probably cannot use federal or state aid (and probably not any private scholarships, either). On the other hand, the tuition may be so much lower that he will not need any aid. Note, however, that if he takes a leave of absence to study abroad through a foreign university, his lenders may demand that he start to repay his student loans.

Study abroad aid is also available from other sources, including fellowships such as the Freeman-Asia Scholarship, which funds undergraduates studying languages in Asian countries.

Bear in mind that financial aid and scholarship deadlines come early. For fall programs, these deadlines tend to cluster in the January and February prior to leaving. (Sites like www.studyabroad.com and www.nafsa .org have extensive listings of study abroad aid.)[1]

*Working Abroad*: Working locally is possible if the student's visa permits it. In some countries students are permitted to work twenty hours per week during term, and either twenty or forty hours per week during vacation periods. The student may need a work permit in addition to a visa or residency permit. Note, too, that a student's earnings abroad will be subject to local (i.e., foreign) taxes as well as American taxes. The advantages of working while abroad may include more than making money. The student may have the opportunity to practice the language and interact with locals. Depending on the nature of the work (with an embassy, for example), the experience may help students as they apply for international scholarships and may become a talking point in an interview. The primary disadvantage is that the time taken for the job might be better spent studying, socializing with locals, or traveling. The student's personal circumstances and those of the job will determine whether working abroad is a good idea.

## Following Up: After Study Abroad

The value fellowships, graduate programs, and employers place on students' experience will depend in large part on how students articulate what they gained and learned from the experience.[2] Their ability to understand and interpret the value of their study abroad will be increased to the extent that they reflect on their experience and analyze the intercultural and other skills they have developed. Fellowships advisors can play an important role in helping students reflect upon their experiences in order to articulate them for inclusion in applications. Consider offering follow-up appointments for individual students, or workshops for several students at a time, that help them answer the following questions:

- How has your study abroad experience affected your view of yourself? Of the United States?
- Which accepted American behaviors now strike you as most problematic? Why?
- What experience abroad best demonstrates how you have changed? How you have developed? Have robust examples available of how you learned to cope, solve problems, appreciate differences, work independently, and so on.
- What experience after your return to the U.S. best demonstrates your development?
- What skills important to your future study or employment have you developed? What experiences demonstrate your development of each skill?

The answers to these questions will come in handy for fellowship application essays and cover letters. In an application and (for the lucky few) with an interview, students should be ready to explain how they benefited from study abroad. They should be able to articulate what influenced their choice, as well as why they lived, worked, and studied the way they did. They should review their transcripts and be able to discuss how individual courses helped them toward their educational and career goals. Study abroad experiences are most rewarding when they are chosen with care, embraced fully, and reflected upon thoughtfully. A winning experience while abroad can certainly contribute to a successful application experience for the student after returning home.

## Note

1. The following websites provide additional searchable databases of study abroad programs and, to varying extents, resources and tools: www.iiepassport .org; www.studyabroaddirectory.com; www.goabroad.com; www.transitions abroad.com; www.iiebooks.org (focuses on study abroad programs available during vacation periods); and www.languagesabroad.com (a language school database).

2. For more on the importance of this kind of reflection, see Karna Walter's essay (chapter 5, this volume).

# 8

## Bela Karolyi's Handstand
### The Whys and Hows of Letters of Endorsement

**DOUG CUTCHINS, DAVID SCHUG, AND MARY DENYER**

---

*Doug Cutchins* is the director of global awards at New York University, Abu Dhabi. Previously, he was the director of social commitment, and then associate dean and director of postgraduate transitions at Grinnell College, positions that he held for a total of fifteen years. Cutchins served in the leadership of NAFA as a member of the board of directors from 2005 to 2009, then as vice president from 2009 to 2011, and president from 2011 to 2013. He also coauthored All Before Them: Student Opportunities and Nationally Competitive Fellowships *as well as four editions of the book* Volunteer Vacations: Short-Term Adventures That Will Benefit You and Others, *and served on the board and as president of both the Grinnell-Newburg (Iowa) School District and the Grinnell, Iowa, United Way. He is a returned Peace Corps volunteer (Suriname, 1995–1997), and holds an MA in history from the University of Connecticut and a BA in history with secondary teaching licensure from Grinnell College.*

---

**David Schug** is the director of the National and International Scholarships Program at the University of Illinois at Urbana-Champaign. His involvement with NAFA extends from the summer of 2002, before even starting his position at Illinois, when he attended a regional conference in Portland, Oregon. He served as a NAFA board member from 2009–2013 before being elected treasurer and leading the Finance Committee from 2013–2015. He earned a BA in International Studies from St. Norbert College and an MA in International Affairs from George Washington University before working four years as a budget analyst for the Wisconsin State Legislature. He has served as a national reviewer for the Boren, Critical Language, and Gilman scholarships.

---

**Mary Denyer** has been the assistant secretary and head of Scholarship Administration of the Marshall Aid Commemoration Commission since 2001. Responsible for the administration of the Marshall Scholarship, her job ranges from drafting policy for the Foreign and Commonwealth Office to the pastoral care of the 100 scholars who are in the UK each year. Denyer has an international perspective in matters related to education and policy, having worked for the Association of Commonwealth Universities for nearly twenty years. She has worked on all four of the largest British government–sponsored scholarships: Marshall, Chevening, Commonwealth, and Fulbright. She has a BA (Hons) in American Studies and History from the University College of Ripon and York St John (University of Leeds) (now York St John University) and a PGDip in Higher and Professional Education from the Institute of Education, University of London (now UCL). She also spent a semester at the University of South Florida, where she was placed on the dean's list for outstanding students. Denyer is also a Fellow of the Royal Society of Arts.

---

Conjure up an image of a gymnastics coach on the sidelines of the Olympics, watching a top athlete on the uneven parallel bars. Think about the hours of practice that coach has put in with the gymnast, discussing possibilities, helping the athlete think through difficult transitions, giving encouragement in the tough moments. The coach knows the gymnast's routine by heart and anticipates where each twist and turn is leading next.

Now imagine that, as a part of the gymnast's score, the coach had to go out on the floor and perform a small piece, too, tumbling about through cartwheels, round offs, and somersaults. At the highest levels, the coach's performance could certainly make a small but important difference, perhaps big enough to impact the final outcome of the competition.

That is, in many ways, how institutional letters of endorsement (sometimes referred to as "nomination letters") operate in scholarship competitions. Yes, the application belongs to the student, who is responsible for its content and ultimately reaps the benefits and recognition (as they should) if the applicant is selected to receive the award. Fellowships advisors rightly walk in the shadows of their students, providing support, guidance, and encouragement, but ultimately the work and the application is theirs.

This is true for all but one element of the application: the letter of endorsement. This piece is the advisor's responsibility and is a special opportunity to help students achieve their goals. Advisors have the chance to practice what they preach and use the advice they dole out to students and their recommenders: *Make the letter easy to read and follow. Catch the eye of someone reading a lot of applications. Show; don't tell.* This task can feel like a tremendous weight and can lead to honest and real struggles, especially for the students fellowships advisors feel most passionately about, or think have the best shot at winning. There is some solace, however, in remembering that the advisor's role is indeed complementary. The best letter of endorsement ever written will not win a scholarship for a sub-par candidate, and the very best candidates will not be sunk by a mediocre letter. In sum, letters of endorsement are our short tumbling routine to complement the student's much larger and more central work.

Letters of endorsement are difficult because they often include an inherent contradiction. Although fellowships advisors are supposed to explain why the institution is nominating this student, foundations generally advise not to repeat information available elsewhere in the application. In other words, tell the foundation why this student is great, but do not use the reasons that the student or letter writers are using. No wonder writing these is a daunting task, a frequent topic of conversation, and a cause of angst in the fellowships advising world.

Only a handful of scholarships and fellowships require a letter of endorsement; most awards allow students to apply directly, without any approval by their home institution. Prominent in this small group that do require letters of endorsement are the Beinecke, Churchill, Marshall, Mitchell, Rhodes, Truman, and Watson scholarships and fellowships. Some other awards require variations on the theme. The Fulbright Campus Committee Evaluation is an institutional endorsement, though not in the form of a letter, and the Schwarzman Scholarship requires a brief letter for candidates who are currently enrolled in bachelor's programs to certify that they will graduate on time (advisors may use the Schwarzman letter to discuss pertinent information not covered elsewhere in the application, but doing so is not required).

Part of the challenge of writing letters of endorsement is that the requirements and prompts vary by foundation. In general, these letters are relatively short, often between 500–1,000 words; explain why, of all available candidates, the institution chose to endorse this student and describe the candidate and the candidate's achievements in the context of the scholarship on offer.

Outside of these general similarities, the requirements for letters, how they are utilized within an application package, the weight given to them, and the topics they should address can vary greatly from award to award. One of the key roles of a fellowships advisor is to get to know each award, its requirements, processes, and preferences, and to give the foundations the information they need to make informed decisions.

By way of illustration, it may prove helpful to review the specific letter of nomination requirements (from their websites) for four foundations.

## Marshall Scholarship

The letter of endorsement is the Institution's opportunity to give the regional committee a deeper insight into the candidate's qualities and potential. Endorsers should indicate how the candidate performed throughout the college or university selection process, and why the institution chose to endorse that candidate. The letter should provide perspective—placing the candidate, the letters of recommendation, and the application in context. It should also outline why and how the candidate best fits the Marshall Scholarship criteria.

The letter of endorsement does not need to repeat what is covered elsewhere in the application and letters of recommendation. The endorsement letter should tell the Regional Committee what they cannot know from the application and recommendation letters.[1]

## Truman Scholarship

Enthusiastic, carefully written letters from Faculty Representatives help good candidates advance to the interview—even if they have one or two weak points. Ordinary letters are a disservice, even to strong candidates.

An effective Faculty Representative Nomination Letter:

- discusses both how the nominee meets selection criteria, in particular stressing his/her leadership and potential to be a "change agent," and how the nominee qualifies as an outstanding representative of the institution [e.g., worthy of being put forward as a student trustee, as a student member of a dean or presidential search committee, or for other positions of exceptional leadership];
- makes the case why this candidate is outstanding in terms of leadership and academics and change-agent potential;
- presents one or two examples of accomplishment or achievement of the candidate;
- explains any apparent weaknesses in the candidacy; and,
- identifies any unusual aspects of the school that might strengthen the candidacy (e.g., strict grading policy, limited opportunities for involvement in internships or in the community).
- While there is no word or character limit for letters of recommendation, the Foundation strongly recommends that letters be confined to two printed pages.[2]

## Watson Fellowship

The nomination letter is submitted by the campus adviser, but it need not be written by the adviser. Some letters are written independently by a specific committee member, while others may be written collectively by the committee. Style, content, and approach may vary; the word count limit is 500 words.

This letter tells us why the campus committee chose this candidate above others from the pool. It describes the candidate's "unusual promise," as seen in the written materials, in the interview, and in any subsequent interactions with the candidate. The nomination letter is commonly read after the Personal Statement and Project Proposal, so it does not need to review these in great detail. The nomination letter serves best as a "yellow highlighter" to emphasize the most important points in the candidate's record that must not be overlooked by the National Selection Committee. Which activities, for example, are most impressive in the context of this specific institution? On different campuses, it may be student government, or an honor council, or community service, or a specific student advocacy club . . . where "movers and shakers" tend to be concentrated. For an outsider, such insight is difficult to discern.

The nomination letter provides a good opportunity to inject information that was revealed during the campus selection process. What red flags did a particular candidate raise, for example, and how did the committee come to terms with them? How did the candidate perform in the campus interview? In preparing for the Watson application, how has a candidate taken on specific challenges, such as refining her topic, confronting difficult personal issues, tracking down contacts, or overcoming specific liabilities?

Some nomination letters include short quotations from others—faculty members, for example, who are not serving as official references—that add further depth and perspective to the application. The nomination letter is an ideal means to reiterate the strengths of the candidate/application and address any liabilities certain to surface for the candidate in the national selection process.[3]

## Beinecke Scholarship

A letter from the dean or administrative officer summarizing the reasons for the nominee's selection.[4] [That is the sum of the instruction.]

In these examples, Marshall is very clear that it does not want a mere recitation of the candidate's main accomplishments and achievements, as these will become evident over the course of the application. Conversely, Truman is much more open to the *Cliffs Notes* version of the candidate's application, noting the main points committee members should look for. The Watson is painstakingly detailed in the information that it wants to see and clear that the letter writer only gets 500 words to fulfill these requirements. Beinecke has the briefest instructions of these four and leaves the content and length of the letter up to the author.

These differences are also reflected in the letter's location within the packet that committee members receive. For example, in the Truman application, the letter of endorsement is the top document, and the first place that the committee meets the student, so a summary of what is to come makes sense. On the other hand, the Marshall letter of endorsement is placed after the résumé information, essays, and transcripts, so the committee members are well aware of the student's accomplishments by the time they read the endorser's letter. These varying placements help explain the different approaches that the letters take in the content that they seek. Smart endorsers learn the differences between what various foundations desire in their letters and write accordingly.

Part of the challenge of writing these letters is that they place the endorser firmly as the intermediary between the candidate and the foundation. On the one hand, institutions are clearly on the side of their applicants. An advisor, often the one drafting the letter, is being paid by the university to help its students compete for awards, so universities, and by extension advisors, have a vested interest in seeing their students succeed and have obvious motivations to present the most polished cases for their candidates. On the other hand, the best advisors build long-term relationships with foundations, accept academic norms and strictures that call for rigor and intellectual honesty in their writing, and endorse the notion that society at large is best served by foundations accepting the "best" candidates without regard to institution. In writing letters of endorsement, then, fellowships advisors have to walk the line between crafting the best narrative for their candidates while also being an honest broker with the foundations.

In thinking about letters of endorsement from the student advocate perspective, one way to conceive of this task is that the fellowships advisor is in effect writing a personal statement on behalf of the student. These letters are often about the same length as the student's personal statement, and the general idea—making sense of this person's life and accomplishments in a limited amount of space, and in an interesting way, to a reader who has never met the student before—is similar as well. The problem for the fellowships advisor, of course, is that the student's personal statement already exists. Because students have already written and explained who they are, writing letters of endorsement can feel repetitive. The key is to reflect and echo the student's personal statement without copying it. The letter of endorsement needs to feel like it is describing the same person that the committee has met or will meet in the personal statement, without repeating what the student has chosen to say. One way to do this is to pick up on the themes and ideas that the student discusses in the personal statement and to amplify this message by telling stories and giving examples that demonstrate these personality traits in other contexts.

At the same time, letters of endorsement can be thought of as a trust-building exercise with the foundation. This is an opportunity to place the candidate squarely within the foundation's selection criteria, especially if the student has not already done so. By understanding the foundation, the characteristics they seek in candidates, and the goals they have for their funding, fellowships advisors can use letters of endorsement to demonstrate that they have done their homework and are nominating appropriate candidates.

In doing so, endorsers should not try to hide or gloss over weaknesses in the candidate's files. Foundations are exceptionally good—almost scarily so—at quickly reading files and finding candidates' weak spots with surgical precision. Some foundations, such as Truman, give feedback on candidates' files, and these conversations bring to mind a master chef filleting a fish, separating the meat from the bone with a speed and accuracy that can be breathtaking. Have no doubt; they will find the candidate's weaknesses. There is no such thing as a flawless candidate. Fellowships advisors may as well admit those weaknesses, and then use the letter to explain why the committee endorsed the candidate anyway.

There is another reason to provide a complete picture of the applicant in these letters of endorsement. If the application is persuasively written, the candidate often will need to meet representatives of the foundation in an interview setting. Do not write checks that candidates cannot cash in an interview or indeed in their scholarship if they win one. If a committee reads a file that describes a candidate as a gregarious leader, known by all on campus, with a penchant for speaking up often in class, that is the person the committee will justifiably expect to meet in the interview room. Letters of endorsement are, then, a good opportunity to set reasonable, verifiable expectations; if an endorser has concerns about a student's performance in front of a committee, those concerns should be stated in the letter of endorsement.

Some of these letters are easy to write. The challenge of writing on behalf of a brilliant, multitalented standout student is often nothing more than finding ways to cram all of the advisor's adulation for that student into a short document. But what of the qualified-but-not-great candidate? The student who checks all of the boxes, but who is uninspiring? The candidate the committee had to discuss at length and eventually decided, "well, there is no reason to withhold a nomination, but the student probably will not come close to an interview, let alone win?" These cases pose challenges exactly because they put fellowships advisors in that precarious intermediary role of wanting to be on the student's side, but also wanting to present the candidate honestly to the foundation. Such cases call for a deft hand, presenting not only the best, but also the most honest case in the letter of endorsement. Do not puff students up to be more than they are, but do showcase their strengths. In the end, foundations will do their job and make the best decision they can about the candidate in the context of the applicant pool.

Letters of endorsement also provide opportunities to help candidates in a few other ways. First, such a letter is a chance to contextualize the candidate's achievements on campus. If the student won the Smith Family Prize, the committee does not know if that is a common award given to half the graduating class for completing ten hours of community service, or a prestigious, campus-wide recognition for the one student who demonstrates the most outstanding academic promise. Second, letters of endorsement are a great place to explain campus quirks that may not make sense anywhere else. Does the real seat of power reside not in student government but in fraternities, and this candidate's presidency of the Pan-Hellenic Council was the most influential role possible? This letter is the place to explain that aspect of campus life. Finally, it is very common that candidates may have one aspect of their lives that is incredibly important to understand in order to have a sense of who they are, but is not easy to include anywhere else in the application. This might be a sibling with special needs, the death of their first-year roommate, a learning disability, or that they were a child actor who had a starring role in a movie. These facts can individualize candidates, adding to well-rounded pictures of who they are and what their stories have been to date.

In writing letters of endorsement, it is of vital importance that endorsers follow the rules set out by the foundation. First, of course, is understanding whether or not a letter is necessary at all. The Udall Foundation annually reminds fellowships advisors that a letter of endorsement is not just unnecessary, but unwelcome, and will be deleted if submitted. Second is to adhere strictly to word counts, which is both important ethically to follow the rules set out by the foundations, and to serve as a model for students under similar restrictions. Third, and most controversial, is to understand who has to sign the letter of endorsement. While most foundations are fine with the fellowships advisor writing and signing the letter, others—chief among them the Marshall—insist on the signature of a senior officer of the school, such as a provost, vice chancellor, or president. Fellowships advisors need to have early conversations with these administrators to agree what the writing process will be, and who will do the heavy lifting of authorship. What is tricky for advisors about this demand is that all parties involved recognize this issue of authorship: the letter is typically not actually written by the person who will sign it. Some NAFA members have raised ethical questions about this ghostwriting. The foundations, for their part, typically note that they recognize that the letters are not written by the signer, but ask for such a signature to demonstrate buy-in to the process at the highest levels. On some campuses, fellowships advisors have threaded the needle on this issue by ensuring that the signatory to the letter meets the candidate for a conversation before signing; by not including first-person endorsements in the letter, deferring instead to "the committee's endorsement of this student," or by co-signing the letter alongside the senior officer.

All of these philosophical frameworks are well and good, but how does the committee member, fellowships advisor, or assistant to the president actually write such a letter? What is the process for producing the letter of endorsement? In writing a successful letter, there are two main factors to keep in mind: collecting information and building the letter into the overall on-campus application endorsement timeline.

Writing an effective letter of endorsement requires, above all, that the endorser knows the student well. Part of this knowledge will come about naturally, over the course of working with the student for (in a best-case scenario) months before the on-campus application deadline. Well-organized fellowships advisors will record notes about the student's application from the first meeting. These notes can include general impressions, but even better are anecdotes, examples, and stories that can eventually be woven into a letter of endorsement. As such, taking copious notes during interviews and committee discussions is always a good idea. What did the student say that impressed the committee? What did your committee members voice about the candidate after the interview? What did the candidate say that could not be found elsewhere in the application?

One way to begin writing such a letter is to read through the candidate's entire application packet and approach the effort organically. What succinct thesis statement might begin to sum up this student's application? What themes emerge regarding this student? The endorser may want to develop an outline of these themes and then look for evidence to help make them real to the reader. Generally, this tends to come from a combination of new information and aspects of the application, reorganized in a way that tells a nuanced story about the applicant. In doing so, review the criteria for the specific award. What are the main points about the candidate that the letter can affirm? An effective letter will consider what might not be evident from the application or other letters of recommendation and will fill that gap.

Some advisors include boilerplate about the institution or the nominating committee in the letter of endorsement. While this may be helpful, doing so can also eat up precious space and does not help differentiate this candidate. National committees are generally less interested in who serves on the committee and find more compelling why that committee chose to nominate this student. Endorsers are wise to use boilerplate sparingly.

Once a student has secured a nomination, the fellowships advisor may wish to have a more structured and intentional conversation with the candidate in order to help inform the letter-writing process. These conversations often last an hour or more and should be conducted in a relaxed setting where candidates are encouraged to talk about their lives, the ideas that animate them, and their chief accomplishments, sharing stories about what makes them who they are. It may be helpful to give the student, in advance, a list of open-ended prompts (as appropriate to the institution and the student), such as:

1. Tell me about your family.
2. Why did you choose to come to this university?
3. What motivates you?
4. Is your success due more to hard work or natural ability?
5. How do you prioritize?
6. Why and how did you choose your major?
7. What has been your most significant leadership activity in college?
8. What accomplishment is your greatest source of pride?
9. How did you spend your summers?
10. What is your social network like?
11. What do you do for fun?
12. What role does faith play in your life?
13. Who do you look up to? Who are your heroes?
14. When do you feel like you are your true self?
15. What does the future hold for you?
16. What motivates you to want to study abroad? (Use for relevant scholarships.)
17. What are your plans if you do not win the scholarship?

The purpose of these prompts is simply to encourage students to open up and talk about different aspects of their lives. Sometimes just looking at this list and thinking about these questions help candidates identify some key aspects of what makes them unique, or the major themes in their life that need to be teased out in the letter of endorsement. The role of the fellowships advisor in this conversation is to be quiet and let the student do all of the talking, while taking detailed notes and keeping the student on track. Students, even millennials, often have a hard time talking about themselves for a full hour, or knowing what is most interesting about their lives. They may try to sidetrack the conversation into how wonderful their organic chem lab partner was (this letter is not about the organic chem lab partner) or go five layers deep on how they organized a photography exhibit (which may get a mention in the letter, but certainly not to that depth). Fellowships advisors should not be afraid to let the student know when the conversation needs to move along or change direction.

These conversations with nominees can be important bonding moments between the fellowships advisor and the student. They often occur at a pivotal moment, generally coming after months of working together, and at a high point, after the students have secured the university's nomination. These can be fun, enjoyable conversations, as the fellowships advisor learns more about these students and thinks about how best to describe these amazing people to others. Because of the nature and length of the exchange, these conversations can often be intense, personal, and revelatory. Fellowships advisors should make certain students know that this is a purposeful conversation, and, unless instructed otherwise, that it is entirely on the record. In fairness, students need to know at the start of the discussion that everything they say is fair game for the letter of endorsement, and that they should explicitly point out anything that they do not want in the letter. On this note, it is worth mentioning that letters of endorsement fall under students' academic records and are therefore subject to FERPA regulations; fellowships advisors should present students with a waiver statement for them to sign before authoring the letter of endorsement, guaranteeing that the letter will remain confidential. If students decline to do so, that information should be mentioned in the letters of endorsement.

One of the best outcomes from such a conversation is a "Golden Nugget": an example, turn of phrase, or anecdote that succinctly and perfectly sums up the student and demonstrates honestly who this student is and what makes this candidate tick. A Golden Nugget is one piece of particularly evocative information that encapsulates the essence of the student. It is probably something that comes completely naturally to the student and may even seem unremarkable, but perhaps is something that nobody else does. A Golden Nugget will stick with committee members after they read it and may even become a defining part of how the committee remembers and refers to the student.

Below are three illustrations:

- Another example of Nicholas's determination is in the weight room. If you had a picture of Nicholas, you would be shocked by this: he's about 5'2" and looks like a strong wind could be problematic for him. But a few years ago he was in the college's weight room with a friend from the football team, who pointed out the record board to him. "And at that moment," he recalls, "I decided I wanted my name up there." He currently holds one weightlifting record and has tied another—but won't allow his name to be put on the board until he actually breaks it, which he intends to do this spring.
- Nathan charmed our committee when he admitted to having a motto for his running; during every run, he chooses either the hardest or the best moment and says out loud, "I love running, I love this university, and life is good." That he finds ways to pick himself up and remind himself how lucky he is speaks volumes of his temperament and attitude toward life.
- Maggie's musical abilities are quite noteworthy. She has played the violin for thirteen years and has attained a high level of competency. Her orchestra conductor describes her abilities in this way: "She is not, in any sophisticated sense, musically educated; she does, however, earnestly love to play, and she plays ingenuously, with candid expressiveness and obvious gratification. That sort of thing to a conductor is worth any amount of sophistication." Indeed, Maggie has admitted that, late at night in a classroom building, she will take a break from her studies, stand on the table, and play an impromptu concert for herself.

As the third Golden Nugget example above illustrates, bringing in outside voices that are not utilized elsewhere in the student's application can be both helpful and powerful. This may be particularly true in describing the student's academic work: the committee will already see the student's transcript and GPA and usually has at least three academic letters of recommendation, so what else is there for a fellowships advisor—who has probably not taught this student—to say about the student's academic record? Ask students to provide a list of three to eight people whom they considered asking for letters of recommendation but did not, from a range of different experiences, including academics, internship supervisors, coaches, and so on. It may even be appropriate to include the voices of students' peers, depending on the situation. Then, reach out to those people to invite their brief comments, highlighting those anecdotes and stories that are the most useful and insightful. Such a message might look like this:

> *As you may know, Jane Doe is one of our university's nominees in this year's Marshall Scholarship competition, which would fund her study in the UK after graduation. As the university's liaison to the Marshall Foundation, it is my responsibility to write the college's letter of institutional endorsement for Jane. In writing many such letters in the past, I have found it extremely helpful to include comments from other people who know Jane, her abilities, and her accomplishments. The best comments are specific in nature, and often include an anecdote that demonstrates a particular skill or personality trait. If possible, would you be willing to reply to this email by Monday, September 28, with a paragraph or so of your thoughts on Jane? I do not want you to spend too much time on this, and it does not need to be a crafted document. Please do not take the time to write a full letter—a paragraph will definitely suffice. Thank you for your assistance with this as I work with Jane to try to produce the best possible institutional endorsement in support of her application.*

Such outside voices are particularly helpful in demonstrating themes in the student's life across multiple dimensions. If the fellowships advisor describes the student as creative or tenacious or hard-working, and then provides examples from a professor, a coach, and a supervisor showing that aspect of the student's life, the description is much more likely to resonate with the committee.

In describing the student, fellowships advisors should also be aware of the role that implicit bias and stereotypes may play in the language used in the letter. Several recent studies have pointed out the extent to which letter writers often unwittingly use coded or gendered language to describe candidates.[5] These biases are very difficult to overcome, but being aware of them as an obstacle is an important first step. The University of Arizona's Commission on the Status of Women has an excellent one-page handout that may be helpful to review before beginning the writing process.[6] After writing, consider running the text of the letter through British researcher Tom Forth's Gender Bias Calculator,[7] which points out exactly which words in the letter tend to be associated with one gender or another.

Finally, as readers may have surmised, writing letters of endorsement is a time-consuming and lengthy process, and fellowships advisors need to build space into the application process timeline in order to successfully write them. Even after meeting with candidates multiple times, fellowships advisors will want to put the student on notice that they may be asked seemingly random questions, in order to help advisors correctly narrate their story and add value to the application packet. Saving sufficient time for the editorial process is important. On average, letter writers should expect to spend a total of four to six hours per letter over the course of several weeks to gather notes, interview the student, collect anecdotes from others, tease out the themes and structure of the letter, actually write it, revise and edit it, perhaps send it to a senior administrator's office for approval and signature (making sure that the one signing is not out on a fundraising trip at that moment) before uploading it to the system (all while modeling timeliness and not waiting until the last minute to do so). All of this, of course, needs to take place after the nomination occurs, which means that on-campus deadlines, interviews, and nomination decisions need to take place sufficiently early—at least three to four weeks—before the national deadline.

That is a lot of hard work. But by thinking about this task as an opportunity to further get to know exceptional candidates and to help them achieve their dreams as they launch into the world, fellowships advisors may find this as not just an essential, but a rewarding experience.

And it could be worse—at least foundations are not asking us to perform a cartwheel.

## Notes

1. See www.marshallscholarship.org/applications/advisorinfo.
2. See https://truman.gov/2017-notes-faculty-reps.
3. Information sent to Watson institution partners.
4. See fdnweb.org/beinecke/how-to-apply/required-materials.
5. K. Dutt, D. Pfaff, A. F. Bernstein, J. S. Dillard, and C. J. Block, "Gender Differences in Recommendation Letters for Postdoctoral Fellowships in Geoscience." *Nature Geoscience*, 9 (2016): 805–808.
6. Available at http://www.csw.arizona.edu/sites/default/files/csw_2015–10 –20_lorbias_pdf_0.pdf.
7. Available at http://www.tomforth.co.uk/genderbias.

# Part III

## Expanding Opportunity

# 9

# Widening the Pool
## Assessing Campus Diversity and Making Fellowship Recruitment More Inclusive

## JENNIFER GERZ-ESCANDÓN

*Jennifer Gerz-Escandón is the director of national scholarships and fellowships for the Georgia State University Honors College. She holds a BA in government with a minor in psychology from Georgetown University, an MA in International Relations from the University of Miami, a diploma in International Relations from the University of the West Indies, and a PhD in International Relations from the University of Miami. Her previous roles include associate professor and chair of International Relations and director of the Center for International Programs and Services at Lynn University. Prior to Lynn University, she held the position of director of International Studies and assistant professor of political science at the University of Evansville. A highlight of her more than a dozen years in higher education was a 2001–2002 International Education Administrator Fulbright experience in Germany. Gerz-Escandón is advisor to the Gates Millennium Scholarship Georgia State chapter and regularly serves as a scholarship reader for the Congressional Hispanic Caucus Institute Scholarship Program and the*

*Asian Pacific Islander American Scholarship Fund. She has presented at several NAFA regional workshops, contributed articles to previous volumes, and serves on the NAFA Technology, Publications and Communications Committee.*

---

Thinking of diversity as an American fixation is tempting, but a growing chorus of voices is raising awareness of inclusion—or the dangers of exclusion—globally. This concern is also driving discussions in the fellowships community, a group rarely found on the sidelines of issues having an impact on higher education. In 2016, NAFA hosted regional conferences on diversity in Claremont, California, and Evanston, Illinois. Presentations, workshops, and facilitated discussions on fellowship diversity initiatives covered race, class, and gender; social justice frameworks; communicating diversity; microaggressions; and microcorrections in the advising process, among other topics.

On the other side of the Atlantic, diversity initiatives such as these have a different name. Those studying in the UK are likely familiar with the phrase "widening the pool." It is common parlance for expanding the gender, ethnic, socioeconomic, or experiential diversity of participants in a given pursuit or profession to reflect more accurately the society it serves or, in some cases, the global norms of the professional community of which it is a part. Nearly a decade ago, UK government policymakers began advocating for diversity in professions ranging from financial services and corporate boards to judges according to British broadsheets and ICSA, The Governance Institute based in London.[1]

## A Short History of Diversity in American Higher Education

What does widening the pool entail in the context of higher education and when did it become a matter of concern? In the United States, judicial decisions have moved issues of inclusion into the national spotlight, from the 1954 *Brown v. Board of Education* desegregation decision to the recent 2016 U.S. Supreme Court decision reaffirming the constitutionality and value of considering diversity in university admissions decisions in *Texas v. Fisher*. Colleges and universities are responding by addressing diversity in mission statements and taking stock of what initiatives are working, what communities are being addressed, and whether or not strategic goals are being achieved.

Campus diversity assessment models and tools abound, emphasizing campus composition, processes, and culture. Sylvia Hurtado, a prominent professor of education and director of the Higher Education Research Institute at the University of California, Los Angeles, actively documented the benefits of inclusive campuses, and in her 1998 campus climate model, raised awareness of the effect of race and ethnicity in higher education.[2] Subsequent researchers have looked at broader categories of under-representation in changing university contexts.[3] While Hurtado's traditional definition of diversity focused on race, ethnicity, and gender, more recent definitions have grown to include underrepresented LGBTQ students, low-income students, and students with disabilities.[4] As fellowships advisors, perspectives on diversity are also influenced by the cues taken from the priorities of fellowship programs that may emphasize other aspects of diversity. The U.S. Student Fulbright Program has a stated goal of reflecting the diversity of the country, adding military and veterans, creative and performing artists, and students from geographically rural areas.[5]

In 2005 deeper linkages between diversity and quality, diversity as a process rather than outcome, and diversity as it has an impact on and is affected by organizational culture were explored in a three-part study on Making Excellence Inclusive commissioned by the Association of American Colleges and Universities.[6]

## Diversity and Fellowships

What does widening the pool have to do with the pursuit of national scholarships and fellowships? Some of the most established and competitive awards recently found themselves under fire due to a perceived lack of diversity. Years of demographic data posted annually by the Marshall Commission reveal a conscientious effort to allay such concerns.[7] Some observers worry the portrait of achievement painted by their scholars suggests diversity and excellence do not go hand-in-hand.

Critics wonder whether selection processes and recruitment strategies for some prestigious awards re-create systems of privilege deeply embedded in society, offering a narrow pathway to social mobility for underrepresented high achievers who might benefit most from the opportunities, networks, and funding prestigious fellowships offer. Two sobering reminders counter these concerns: (1) such opportunities reward merit and leadership rather than need for social mobility, and (2) clearly defined eligibility and selection criteria and evaluation processes are designed to ensure equitable outcomes.

## Assessing Applicant Identification and Recruitment

Given these realities, how can fellowships that invite applications from U.S. students of all majors be made more inclusive? The logical place to focus for fellowships advisors, foundations, and organizations is in applicant identification and recruitment. Issues of representation in award outcomes can be addressed through more intentional inclusiveness in the identification and recruitment of potential applicants. This essay examines the role fellowships advisors and fellowship sponsors can and do play in diversifying the pool of applicants for national scholarships and fellowships. The essay identifies formal frameworks for assessing campus diversity and provides targeted questions to guide an informal assessment of diversity in fellowship recruitment at a campus or program and a nationwide collection of relatively low-cost, field-tested potential applicant identification and recruitment strategies.

An informal assessment of diversity should begin by focusing on diversity on campus and the role it plays in fellowships work. Consider the following three questions: (1) Is campus diversity information regarding not just composition but also campus climate and equity measures scorecard (for an example, see https://www.aacu.org/node/12607) and how do they fit within the institution's overall strategic plan? (2) Are there specific ways campus diversity has an impact on the role of fellowships advisors? (3) What priorities must be addressed in an annual report?

Diversifying the applicant pool may be simply an opportunity or it may be an imperative. Part of the assessment must include approaches to student recruitment and identification. One way to start is to determine the three most effective strategies for identifying well-qualified applicants. Patterns born out of habit might allow unintentional bias or omissions. Next, which campus partners are involved most often? Think about which campus partners are key to building an applicant pool and how to effectively leverage (and show appreciation for) partners' insight. If current strategies are not having the desired results, it is time to dig deeper or branch out.

The final step in the informal assessment entails reviewing obstacles to inclusion. Where are some of the campus gates limiting student identification? Volunteering to read scholarship applications for the admissions office may take the pressure off overworked staff and provide access to a top student whose goal of overcoming the challenges of cerebral palsy and becoming a filmmaker in Ireland puts her in a potential Mitchell Scholarship applicant pool. What are some of the reliable areas that produce applicants in the campus recruitment processes? If the most consistent pool of Rhodes Scholarship applicants comes from the STEM fields, communicating that message to those department chairs may lead to an invitation to address the faculty.

Diversifying the applicant pool can be limited by award criteria and institutional enrollment. Identifying STEM candidates at an arts-focused institution or Pell-eligible students at campuses with high median socioeconomic enrollment will clearly be met with challenges, but it is not impossible. In broadening diversity, enrollment plays a disproportionately important role. If, for example, the percentage of LGBTQ students, students with disabilities, or students who are active military or veterans is not significant, achieving diversity may mean emphasizing a diversity of perspective and experience in other ways. In a 2005 Association of American Colleges and Universities study titled "Making Diversity Work on Campus: A Research-based Perspective," the authors propose a "conception of diversity as a process toward better learning rather than an outcome."[8] Seeking students who have experienced a transformative curriculum that "engages diversity in service to learning" is recommended.[9] A fellowship recruitment tweak might involve collaborating with the international programs office to identify returning study abroad students or meeting with faculty to learn who is taking active learning courses on civil rights, gender issues, or social justice. There are also institutional scholarship programs on many campuses that provide support for underrepresented students. Partnering with these programs can also help locate competitive applicants from diverse backgrounds. What made them attractive for a campus scholarship might also make them successful as a nationally competitive awards candidate.

## Inclusive Micro-Corrections Strategies

For competitive, merit-based, postgraduate scholarships, open to students of all majors, it is possible to make small changes to traditional identification approaches that yield significant inclusive results—a micro-corrections approach. On a college campus, the micro-corrections approach assumes that a national scholarships and fellowships program has established an infrastructure, outreach plan, consistent programming, well-developed communication channels and policies, and procedures. The notion of small changes implies the existence of defined standard operating procedures as a basis for expanding potential applicant reach and building new inroads to include underrepresented potential applicants. A group of fellowships advisors with programs meeting the above criteria agreed to share their strategies for diversifying the applicant pool and identification process for endorsed awards as part of an informal survey.

A survey of fellowships practitioners reveals a variety of diversity-enhancing strategies. For Jeff Portnoy, associate dean of the Honors Program at Perimeter College, a two-year unit of Georgia State University, being a faculty member significantly aids his recruitment and identification strategies.[10] By recruiting potential applicants to take honors courses, he can directly build relationships and demonstrate that he is eager to invest in them. When he is not teaching, he is a fixture at student clubs and regularly attends campus events that matter to students. For Portnoy successful recruitment of first-generation and nontraditional students hinges on students feeling wanted.[11]

Last year Kristen Walton struck gold as a faculty member and fellowships advisor at Salisbury State in Maryland.[12] She connected with underrepresented students by creatively leveraging her relationship with other faculty members. Walton created an invitation to visit her office and asked 400 colleagues to share it with just one student. The 20–25 percent response rate was significant, Walton noted, adding that 75 percent of potential applicants she met as part of this initiative "had never even heard of fellowships and many of them were first-generation or students of color."[13] Walton's creativity carried over into one of her far-sighted identification strategies. Knowing that work-study students have a high financial need, she recruited several to become ambassadors for her office. Walton sees these students as potentially increasing her applicant pool because they learn about the fellowship process early in their academic careers.

Two experienced fellowships advisors at large public research institutions on opposite coasts found ways to circumvent traditional barriers keeping community college students from learning about prestigious scholarships. Alicia Hayes, scholarships/fellowships advisor at the University of California, Berkeley, and Lauren Chambers, assistant director, Office of National Scholarships at the University of South Florida (USF), make a habit of traveling to community colleges or satellite campuses to promote prestigious scholarships. Hayes maintains an unusually strong recruitment network featuring more than a dozen campus and community partners. Based in Tampa, Chambers enjoys significant compositional diversity in the Gulf Coast student population primarily composed of Hispanic, Caribbean, and African American students.[14] USF also leads the nation in Pell Grant recipients.[15] Though the abundance of diverse students offers ample recruitment opportunities, floating between three campuses potentially enhances early identification opportunities and inclusion in a national scholarship pipeline.

Georgia College National Scholarships Office's assistant director Anna Whiteside previously served as fellowships advisor at North Carolina A&T, a STEM-focused, research-oriented institution. Transitioning from an 80 percent African American student body to an 84 percent white liberal arts–focused environment meant significant changes in compositional diversity, perceived campus climate, and who was considered a multicultural student.[16] Multicultural outreach at A&T targeted Latino and LGBTQ students. On both campuses, faculty members prove to be critical partners in identifying applicants for the fellowship pool. Whiteside also partners with alumni from underrepresented groups who are powerful voices in reducing anxiety about applying for competitive study abroad scholarships, particularly for awards like Fulbright. She notes that "Native Americans, Hispanic Americans, and African Americans are still underrepresented in study abroad, and this makes going abroad even more daunting for students from these groups at A&T." Incorporating alumni into the recruitment process allowed Whiteside's nervous students "to have frank discussions with former students who had good experiences abroad."[17]

In all cases, the fellowship recruitment and identification strategies represent relatively straightforward course corrections with the potential for major impacts on applicant pool diversity. The following questions seem obvious, but how many fellowships offices use them to reflect on the process: (1) Who is invited to the applicant pool party? and (2) What could be done (differently) to welcome diverse applicants and support inclusion? Work must be intentional and systematized to become effective over the long term.

## A Fellowship Sponsor's Perspective on Inclusive Fellowship Recruitment

Recruiting outreach from the fellowship organizations and foundations is equally important to diversifying applicant pools. Lee Rivers, the outreach specialist for the Institute of International Education (IIE), supports outreach programs and recruitment for the Fulbright U.S. Student Program, the Gilman International Scholar Program, and the Boren Awards. Rivers, who has served in the role for eight years and visited more than 200 campuses, believes it is essential for the rich diversity of the United States to be well represented abroad through IIE student programs.[18] In his assessment, global problems arise from misunderstandings. Therefore, people-to-people interaction, working and living together, is a good way to solve world issues. The best way to see the diversity that is the United States is to travel the country as he has, visiting approximately 40 states.[19]

The three most effective recruitment strategies Rivers uses include leveraging personal connections, connecting with faculty, and enhanced campus visits. Advisors intent upon building an inclusive pool of fellowship applicants should be aware of key campus collaborators including the disability, career, and multicultural offices. Second, Rivers believes faculty members play an essential role because they have the most face time with students. Faculty need not know the ins and outs of national fellowships and scholarships; they simply need one piece of general encouragement, which can lead students to challenge themselves. Students come and go, Rivers notes, but the faculty remains a long-term, dependable partner.

Finally, IIE also uses a big tent approach, bringing students, faculty senate leaders, department heads, provosts, and presidents together for lunch with study abroad, disability, and career service professionals to ask about the university's international mission and offer ways to assist in advancing it. IIE representatives also share best practices from other campuses. By gathering a broad group of stakeholders together over lunch, Rivers can demystify the awards process, dispel notions that such awards are elitist, and explain what IIE means by recruiting a diverse applicant pool.[20] Enhanced campus visits also provide access to a range of campus gatekeepers, though Rivers relies heavily on Fulbright Program Advisors (FPAs) to establish community and open the doors to lesser-known communities. A strong partnership and clear understanding of each other's priorities benefits both fellowships advisors and sponsors equally and can lead to a more inclusive applicant pool.

## Summary

Widening the framework for understanding how diversity and national fellowships intersect is important if scholarship pools are to be more inclusive. The proposed frameworks, assessment tools, and effective practices from fellowships advisors and fellowship sponsors are intended to assist advisors as they reflect on the inclusiveness of their fellowship applicant pool. Advisors need to take time to review manually collected data and ask: (1) What are the university's, and therefore the fellowships office's, diversity goals? (2) Who is selected for endorsed scholarship and fellowships applicant pools? and (3) What more can be done differently to engage first-generation and underrepresented potential scholarship applicants, where small changes in the modus operandi may produce significant results in the applicant pool?

For most institutions, students who apply successfully for nationally competitive scholarships are highly visible. Widening the applicant pool to include greater diversity increases underrepresented student visibility and helps assert the importance of inclusion for colleges and universities, as well as fellowship sponsors, supporting the inclusive missions of these institutions and helping reinforce their goals in tangible ways. In *Beyond Winning: National Scholarship Competitions and the Student Experience*, the authors (all foundation representatives at that time) stress the importance of being more inclusive:

> *As citizens in societies concerned with merit, we believe that talent is broadly, even randomly, distributed, but only selectively developed. Because many able, talented people have not had the privilege of selective development—experiences that make candidates more attractive and available to those who select them—we are concerned that we may be missing many qualified individuals often from groups underrepresented in many ways in our societies. Missing their potential contributions deprives not only them but all of us as well.*[21]

This idea has been expressed in a variety of ways, but unless real action is taken we will continue to be deprived of those contributions. Recruiting applicant pools that reflect inclusion and excellence is a shared responsibility, which requires collaborative partnerships and creative thinking. Proactively encouraging diversity is also an imperative given the changing U.S. higher education enrollment demographics. Implementing big tent identification strategies for fellowship recruiters on all sides of the fellowship enterprise can widen the pool of recruitment and identification resources and welcome applicant diversity.

## Notes

1. See British calls for diversity in Bob Sherwood, "Diversity: Widening the Gene Pool," *Financial Times*, May 3, 2007, https://www.ft.com/content /303d8924-f7f6-11db-baa1-000b5df10621; Owen Bowcott, "Lady Hale: Supreme Court Should Be Ashamed If Diversity Does Not Improve," *The Guardian*, November 6, 2015, https://www.theguardian.com/law/2015/nov/06/lady -hale-supreme-court-ashamed-diversity-improve; and Henry Ker, "News Digest 4/11/16: Review Calls for End to All-White Boards," *ICSA: The Governance Institute,* November 4, 2016, https://www.icsa.org.uk/knowledge/governance-and -compliance/news-digest/november-2016-review-calls-for-end-to-all-white -boards.

2. Sylvia Hurtado and Rona Halualani, "Diversity Assessment, Accountability, and Action: Going Beyond the Numbers" (Association of American Colleges and Universities, 2014), https://www.aacu.org/diversitydemocracy/2014/fall /hurtado-halualani.

3. Damon A. Williams, *Strategic Diversity Leadership: Activating Change and Transformation in Higher Education* (Sterling, VA: Stylus Publishing, 2013), 18–20.

4. See definitions offered by the California State University website: http://teachingcommons.cdl.edu/mhap/UnderrepresentedStudents.htm, and Noah Baron, "The Forgotten Minorities," *Huffington Post*, May 25, 2011,

http://www.huffingtonpost.com/noah-baron/the-forgotten-underrepres_b
_620995.html.

    5. See U.S. Student Fulbright Program Diversity Policy: https://us
.fulbrightonline.org/about/eligibility.

    6. "Committing to Equity and Inclusive Excellence: A Campus Guide for
Self-Study and Planning, American Association of American Colleges and Universities" (April 2005), 1–11.

    7. Marshall Scholarship Competition Statistics: http://www.marshall
scholarship.org/about/statistics.

    8. Jeffrey F. Milem, Mitchell J. Chang, and Anthony Lising Antonio, "Mak-
ing Diversity Work on Campus: A Research-Based Perspective" (Association of
American Colleges and Universities, 2005), iv–16.

    9. Ibid.

    10. Jeffery Portnoy, in discussion with author, June 14, 2016.

    11. Ibid.

    12. Kristen Walton, email message to author, June 15, 2016.

    13. Ibid.

    14. Lauren Chambers, in discussion with author, June 24, 2016.

    15. See the U.S. Department of Education Web page: https://www2.ed.gov
/finaid/prof/resources/data/pell-institution.html.

    16. Anna Whiteside, email message to author, June 14, 2016.

    17. Ibid.

    18. Lee Rivers, in discussion with author, December 14, 2016.

    19. Ibid.

    20. To review an Institute of International Education assessment of strategic
diversity initiative impact on the Gilman, Boren, and Freeman-Asia scholarships,
see "Current Trends in U.S. Study Abroad and the Impact of Strategic Diversity
Initiatives: Meeting America's Global Education Challenge," White Paper #1
(2007).

    21. Alice Stone Ilchman, Warren F. Ilchman, and Mary Tolar, "Strengthening
Nationally Competitive Scholarships: Thoughts from an International Confer-
ence in Bellagio." *Beyond Winning: National Scholarship Competitions and the
Student Experience* (Fayetteville: University of Arkansas, 2005), 65–88.

# 10

## Belonging, Impostor Phenomenon, and Advising Students from Underrepresented Backgrounds

**BRANDY SIMULA**

---

*Brandy Simula is a postdoctoral fellow at Emory University. She previously served as an academic advisor (2011–2012) and assistant director (2014–2016) for the National Scholarship and Fellowship program at Emory University. She holds a BA degree from Appalachian State University and a PhD from Emory University in Women's Gender and Sexuality Studies, with a concentration in sociology. She is currently working with Emory University's Quality Enhancement Plan, "The Nature of Evidence," which encourages and helps first-year students engage with issues of evidence inside and outside the classroom.*

---

Trained as a sociologist of inequalities, I came to fellowships advising with a deep curiosity about the role of fellowships advisors in dismantling or maintaining the structures of inequality that pervade our social world.[1] In this essay, I draw on the social psychological literature on sense of belonging and impostor phenomenon[2] among students from historically underrepresented backgrounds,[3] as well as my own experience as a fellowships advisor, to describe some of the challenges for fellowships advisors committed to serving students from underrepresented backgrounds and to outline some possible strategies for navigating those challenges.

## Legacies of Inequality and Underrepresentation

Many of the most prestigious and widely recognized scholarships and fellowships—like the academy itself—have alumni rosters that are heavily populated with white, able-bodied, heterosexual, cis-gendered, continuing-generation men from middle-to-upper-class backgrounds. These legacies of institutional and structural privilege significantly shape our students' experiences of higher education at all levels from access itself to micro-interactional, everyday experiences, like not being addressed by preferred pronouns or having their names pronounced incorrectly. Although there are myriad meaningful differences in the experiences of students across groups traditionally underrepresented in the academy, there are also important points of commonality in the conditions that perpetuate inequality and create barriers to full inclusion in the life of the academy, including in competitions for prestigious awards.

## Belonging

For students from historically underrepresented backgrounds, the question "Do I belong here?" can profoundly shape their experiences of higher education, and the literature indicates that students from underrepresented backgrounds are much more likely to question whether they belong than are students who have been historically well represented in higher education.[4] A sense of "belonging" to a community—a feeling that the community is welcoming, affirming, and supportive[5] is strongly positively correlated with academic performance and retention, as well as with better mental health outcomes and higher self-esteem.[6]

Feelings of "not belonging" are common among students from a wide range of underrepresented backgrounds, including first-generation students,[7] students from low-income backgrounds,[8] students of color[9]—particularly African American[10] and Latinx[11] students—women,[12] and students with disabilities.[13] A sense of not belonging among students from underrepresented backgrounds results from experiences of intolerance, social exclusion, and pressure to conform to stereotypes, and students from underrepresented backgrounds report less positive perceptions of campus climate and a weaker sense of community at their institutions in comparison with students from populations historically well represented in higher education.[14] Students from underrepresented backgrounds are both more likely to ask themselves "Do I really belong here" *and* to perceive the answer to that question as "no," in comparison with students from populations historically well represented in the academy.

## Impostor Phenomenon

A sense of not *really* belonging is also a frequent component of impostor phenomenon—also known as impostorism and impostor syndrome—which is a common part of the college experience for students from a wide variety of backgrounds, but is present at much higher rates among students from underrepresented backgrounds, including women,[15] African American,[16] Asian American,[17] and Latinx[18] students. Although research has not investigated the presence of impostor phenomenon among all groups underrepresented in the academy, the processes that underlie impostor phenomenon are common to experiences of groups that are underrepresented in their respective educational and/or professional settings, which suggests that members of other underrepresented groups, such as first-generation students, students with disabilities, and LGBTQ students, may also be especially vulnerable to impostor phenomenon.

Impostor phenomenon—a feeling of "phoniness" among high-achieving students—leads these students to seriously underestimate their own intelligence and competence.[19] Impostor phenomenon creates difficulty internalizing success.[20] Thus, students who feel like impostors attribute their achievements to factors not related to their own ability. These students may feel that their achievements (e.g., being admitted to a prestigious institution, receiving a scholarship or award) are matters of luck, being in the right place at the right time, or due to exceptionally hard work.[21] Students who perceive themselves as impostors are quick to dismiss praise and to question the accuracy of positive evaluations of their intelligence and competence.[22]

Impostor phenomenon creates an intense fear of being exposed as a fraud, and an equally intense fear of failure. Fear of failure leads to heightened apprehension in settings in which achievements, intelligence, and competence are being implicitly or explicitly evaluated.[23] Impostor phenomenon also leads those who experience it to believe they are continually in danger of having their accomplishments exposed as fraudulent.[24] In other words, impostor phenomenon leads those experiencing it to the constant feeling that the answer to "Do I belong here?" must—all evidence to the contrary—*really* be "no."

## Strategies for Serving Students from Underrepresented Backgrounds

Given that students from underrepresented backgrounds frequently struggle with questions of belonging as well as with impostor phenomenon, how do advisors best reach and serve students who may be questioning whether or not they should be at college, much less whether they should apply for prestigious awards? In the sections that follow, I share some strategies for serving students from underrepresented backgrounds.

## Educating Ourselves

One of the primary ways advisors can serve students from underrepresented backgrounds is by educating themselves about the histories and legacies of discrimination and inequality in higher education, about the contemporary features of discrimination and inequalities, and how students from underrepresented groups themselves are working to end inequities in higher education. While it is certainly important to be educated specifically in reference to the underrepresented groups that may be predominantly served by our institutions, it is also important to understand the challenges faced by students from underrepresented groups that may not be a particular focus of our institution. For those students, experiences of isolation may be particularly strong. Understanding the specificities of historical and contemporary experiences of students from a range of underrepresented backgrounds can help an advisor better understand the values and concerns that students may bring to these conversations.

Crucial to this process is the recognition that the challenges and successes of students from underrepresented backgrounds are not necessarily similar. The challenges faced, for instance, by a woman majoring in astrophysics may be quite dissimilar to those faced by a first-generation student interested in pursuing law.

Although discrimination and inequality are unfortunately common experiences for students from underrepresented backgrounds, the specific forms that those experiences take are often significantly different. The questions a gender-nonconforming or trans student may be considering about self-presentation in an interview setting may be quite different from the anxieties a first-generation student may feel about navigating the unfamiliar social setting of an evening reception at a selection weekend. This is, of course, not to imply that all trans or gender-nonconforming students wrestle with questions of self-presentation or that all first-generation students are concerned about their abilities to navigate reception-style events, but to note that the ability to think about and anticipate the range of questions and needs that students may bring is an important part of the advisor's work.

In addition to learning more about the experiences, concerns, and interests of students from underrepresented backgrounds, advisors can also serve students from those backgrounds as they continue to expand awards and opportunities by being particularly attentive to those focused on diversity and underrepresentation, as well as those that may not be specifically targeted toward students from those populations, but that emphasize diversity and/or underrepresentation in the selection process. This includes ensuring that scholarship advisors have an accurate understanding of how diversity is defined across a broad range of awards, as well as a realistic understanding of the relationship between the diversity goals of an award or foundation and the diversity represented among recipients. If scholarship offices advise on a select set of awards, ensuring that many of these types of awards are among those included is critical. Regardless of whether such offices are set up to advise on a select set of awards or to serve a more generalized advising function, being knowledgeable about a broad range of opportunities for students from a diverse set of backgrounds can help advisors connect students with opportunities that are a strong fit for their interests, backgrounds, and accomplishments. This may mean, for example, creating databases of awards searchable by identities or demographic characteristics or creating handouts or flyers highlighting awards focused on particular demographic groups.[25]

Being informed on a broad range of awards that support students from underrepresented backgrounds involves not only learning the specifics of the selection process, but also building an understanding of the award experience for students. I have often had students interested in a specific award ask me whether a black or queer student from our institution had ever received the award, and if so, what hir/her/his experience had been like. Being knowledgeable about what the on-the-ground experience of opportunities are like for students from a variety of backgrounds is a critical part of advising responsibilities. It may be the case that a student from a background similar to that of the student being advised may *not* have previously been a recipient from our institution. In those circumstances, an advisor might need to be more creative in thinking about how to connect the advisee with useful information. That might mean connecting the student with a previous recipient of an award similar in the opportunity it provides and its selection process and criteria or reaching out through the NAFA listserv to colleagues at other institutions who might be able to share the experiences of a recipient from their institution who has a similar background. The important point is that when the student wants to know whether someone like hir/her/himself has ever previously been a recipient at the institution, even if the answer is "no," the advisor can still find ways to connect that student with the information ze/she/he is seeking. By becoming better informed and being creative in how to seek information and make connections, advisors can help show highly qualified students—even if they are in fact the first from their particular demographic group at the institution to apply—that they do indeed "belong" in the pool of highly qualified applicants for that award.

## Language, Visibility, and Representation

One of the most important ways that scholarship advisors can reduce the likelihood that students from underrepresented backgrounds will wonder whether they "belong" in fellowships programs, offices, and processes is by making visible the opportunities for and successes of students from a diverse range of underrepresented backgrounds. For instance, do general program brochures focus on diversity? Do the images of past recipients reflect a diverse range of backgrounds? This may require creative thinking if the previous award recipients are populated heavily by students from traditional backgrounds. Such images can shape the impressions of the office students initially form. If visiting a fellowships office requires students to walk past images of previous recipients that include few or no students from underrepresented backgrounds, then students who are from these backgrounds may (simply from this experience) immediately form a sense of whether or not the office serves students like them, and whether or not they are "like" other students who receive prestigious awards. Because students from underrepresented backgrounds may be less likely to think of themselves as "fellowship material" in comparison to students from backgrounds well represented in the academy, being intentional in the public image we craft for our offices, and in the visuals that we select to represent our offices, can play an important role in whether or not students from underrepresented backgrounds see our offices as ones that serve students like themselves.

Issues of language and visibility matter in every aspect of an advisor's work. Do advisors use inclusive language on our intake forms when asking how applicants self-identify in terms of demographic categories and backgrounds? Do the visual materials of the program include a diverse range of students from underrepresented backgrounds? Do advisors ask for preferred pronouns on intake forms or in initial advising sessions and use them consistently? Do they ensure that the locations of events are accessible? Is the language inclusive in publicity materials and at events? Is it inclusive for a diverse range of students of color? Do advisors use gender-neutral language in guidelines provided on professional dress for interviews? Is there information on accommodations in materials and announcements?

Being attentive to the ways that unconscious and implicit biases may slip into language, from casual conversations with advisees to formal letters of institutional nomination, matters significantly, not only in creating a sense of belonging, but also in selection outcomes. For instance, recommendation letters written for women are two and a half times as likely to use language that makes a minimal rather than strong endorsement.[26] Advisors can be trained to recognize their unconscious patterns of using language that focuses on the efforts rather than accomplishments of students—an unconscious bias toward which some may be prone when describing students from underrepresented or disadvantaged backgrounds. Advisors can also be attentive about what information is shared about students' personal and family backgrounds in letters of nomination and endorsement. Part of the role of advisors is to understand and help students understand if and how it is appropriate to address diversity or challenge in the context of the specific award for which ze/she/he is applying. It is also critical to not intentionally or unintentionally disclose information that students do not wish to have shared. This means erring on the side of caution and not assuming that information students may have shared with us is information they are comfortable with our sharing with selection committees.

We are all—despite our best intentions—imperfect, and this means that we will unavoidably make choices in language and/or actions that are implicitly or explicitly noninclusive or even discriminatory. Learning to recognize our own biases can help us minimize those moments, but they will happen. Owning them publicly and correcting our mistakes can be an important teaching moment. Particularly for students struggling with impostor phenomenon, seeing accomplished people who are "like them" make mistakes, get it wrong, and so on, can be an important part of the process of shifting away from the heightened sense of required perfectionism so many of our students face. This is not to advocate intentionally getting things wrong, of course, but it *is* to suggest that sharing our own personal experiences of failure and mistakes may be an important part of our work in advising students struggling with the fear of making a mistake and being unmasked as being an intellectual phony who does not really belong.

## Making Our Offices and Ourselves Visible

While being intentional in attempts to shape initial impressions of an office is key to drawing in students from underrepresented backgrounds, no matter how accessible and inclusive advisors try to make their offices, the reality is that significant proportions of high-achieving students from underrepresented backgrounds do not think of themselves as potential applicants for prestigious awards, and this means being creative and using multipronged outreach and recruitment strategies in order to reach these students. While advisors might hold informational sessions specifically focused on awards for students from underrepresented and diverse backgrounds, the effects of impostor phenomenon make it less likely that students experiencing it will self-identify as potential applicants for those awards, and thus less likely that those students will attend sessions sponsored by our offices.

There are multiple strategies available to help reach students who might not see themselves as potential candidates for prestigious awards. Holding some advising hours in campus centers that serve students from particular backgrounds—for instance the Latinx Student Center or the LGBTQ House—is one possible method of making an office more visible to students who might not otherwise attend information sessions or office hours, particularly if offices are in remote campus locations, or in locations students might not otherwise visit (for example, in Administrative Affairs offices).[27] Partnering with groups and organizations on campus that serve students from underrepresented backgrounds can help reach students who might not show up at information sessions otherwise. While it can be useful to hold cosponsored sessions with, for example, the Black Student Association, or the Center for LGBTQ Life, it can be equally—and sometimes *more*—useful to give a brief presentation or introduction at a regular meeting or event held by such groups and organizations. Having a brief (five- to ten-minute) overview of fellowships offices we can give at regular meetings of groups that serve students from underrepresented backgrounds can help advisors connect with students that might otherwise be missed.

The work of advisors involves building relationships—with students, faculty, foundation officers, staff from other offices, and colleagues on campus. When we are thinking about building relationships with students from underrepresented backgrounds, making ourselves accessible and visible across a range of settings can be a particularly compelling way of demonstrating a commitment to, and interest in working with, students who belong to particular populations. If the campus has mentoring programs for students from underrepresented backgrounds, getting involved is an excellent way to make connections. Doing so provides an opportunity to build relationships with students, but also an opportunity to network with colleagues who are committed to the success of those students, and who could be excellent referral sources. Similarly, if the campus has programs that identify allies and safe spaces—for example, LGBTQ allies or safe spaces for sexual assault survivors—advisors can take advantage of those as well. Advisors can also—if a campus does not have a program that serves specific populations of students underrepresented on the campus—collaborate with colleagues to organize those programs or events. Being visible in spaces that serve students from underrepresented backgrounds and making a commitment to underrepresented students visible in the program's own physical space are among the many ways to signal to students from underrepresented backgrounds that they do indeed belong, both on the campus in general and in the scholarships and fellowships programs more specifically.

## Advising Students from Underrepresented Backgrounds

For all scholarship and fellowship applicants, regardless of background, the process of writing an application for a prestigious award involves intense grappling with questions of identity and personal narrative: Who am I? What are my accomplishments? What will my future be? These questions, and the process of wrestling with them explicitly in writing, may be particularly fraught for students who are already questioning their sense of belonging, and who may also be struggling with feelings of intellectual phoniness. Talking openly with students about the challenges—and rewards—of wrestling with these questions can be an important part of framing the process for our students as a productive rather than intimidating one.

Advisors can also play a crucial role in helping students identify their achievements. Every fellowships advisor I know has had experiences working with overly modest students who do not consider themselves to be leaders or to have accomplished anything extraordinary, only to have incredible achievements drawn out by careful inquiry. Students from underrepresented backgrounds, particularly first-generation students, may not be familiar with the norms and guidelines that govern academic and professional achievements. Students struggling with impostor phenomenon may be less likely to count their publications, leadership, and research experiences, as such, particularly if they are collaborative or limited to campus-based awards, publications, or organizations. Advisors can be cognizant of these realities in how we have conversations with students about their accomplishments and interests. We can, for example, ask not "Do you have any publications?" but "Are you an author on any publications or posters or have you made a presentation by yourself or with a group?" Asking students what things they spend significant amounts of time on on a weekly or monthly basis can help draw out instances of leadership or service that advisees themselves may consider to be "just helping out." We can also, through conversations with students who spend significant amounts of time working to put themselves through school, help our advisees identify instances of leadership in their work. These conversations are obviously part of the advising process with all of our students, but they can be particularly important for students from underrepresented backgrounds struggling with impostor phenomenon who undervalue their own accomplishments and experiences.

Advisors can also be cognizant of the reality that the pressures created by application processes may be more intense for students from underrepresented backgrounds. For students struggling with impostor phenomenon, the fear of failure may be particularly intense, and we can directly acknowledge those fears. Advisors can help students see the process of applying for a prestigious award as a learning process—one that helps them develop their skills at crafting personal and professional narratives, researching opportunities of interest, and deepening relationships with their mentors. Helping students see the application process as one of personal growth, and one that presents challenges to *all* applicants—no matter how intelligent or accomplished—is one of the key tasks advisors face in helping students from underrepresented backgrounds see themselves as "belonging" among applicants for prestigious awards.

As fellowships advisors committed to serving students from underrepresented backgrounds, our work involves not simply connecting interested students with awards that are a strong match for their interests and skills, but instead a much more holistic process of helping students wrestle with their experiences, achievements, and identities, and this is often especially true in our work with students from underrepresented backgrounds. Of course, not all students from underrepresented backgrounds struggle with impostor phenomenon or a sense of not belonging, but the much higher prevalence of these issues among students from underrepresented backgrounds in comparison with their prevalence among students from backgrounds historically well represented in the academy make it important for advisors to understand and take these issues into account. Educating ourselves about the experiences of students from underrepresented backgrounds, being intentional in issues of representation and our choices of language, and seeking out opportunities to get involved with and help support students from underrepresented backgrounds can help make our offices and campuses more welcoming to students from a variety of underrepresented backgrounds and help contribute to increasing our students' feelings of belonging both on our campuses and among applicants for prestigious awards.

## Notes

1. I want to thank Emily Daina Šaras for productive conversations about the use of the sociological imagination in understanding inequalities in relation to our work as fellowships advisors as we prepared for and gave the workshop, "Fellowships and Social Justice Frameworks: (In)Active Roles of Fellowships Advisors in the Replication of Societal Disprivilege in Higher Education," at the NAFA summer 2016 regional conference in Claremont, California. I am also grateful to my colleagues Megan Friddle and Cathryn Johnson for conversations about combatting impostor phenomenon in our advising and mentoring work and to the many NAFAns who shared their strategies for working with underrepresented students at our summer 2016 conference in Claremont.

2. Importantly, while feelings of not belonging are often associated with impostor phenomenon, students from underrepresented backgrounds often feel a sense of disbelonging even in the absence of impostor phenomenon. That is, even students from underrepresented backgrounds who feel a strong sense of confidence in their intellectual and academic abilities frequently report feeling that they do not belong on their campuses—a feeling of being dissimilar to and/or unwelcome by other members of their campus community.

3. In addition to students of color, first-generation students, students with disabilities, LGBTQ students, gender-nonconforming, trans, and queer students, I include women in the broad category of students from historically underrepresented backgrounds. While women have earned more bachelor's degrees in comparison with men since the early 1980s, the legacy of historical underrepresentation persists in shaping the experience of women in higher education.

4. Julio Frenk, "Why We Need a 'Scholarship of Belonging,'" *The Chronicle of Higher Education 62*(36) (2016), http://www.chronicle.com/article/Why-We-Need-a-Scholarship-/236443.

5. Shannon Williams and Joseph Ferrari, "Identification Among First-Generation Citizen Students and First-Generation College Students: An Exploration of School Sense of Community," *Journal of Community Psychology 43*(3) (2015): 377–387.

6. Julie Ancis, William Sedlacek, and Jonathan Mohr, "Student Perceptions

of Campus Cultural Climate by Race," *Journal of Counseling and Development* 78(2) (2000): 180–185. Williams and Ferrari, "Identification Among First-Generation Citizen Students."

7. Patrick Terenzini, Leonard Springer, Patricia Yaeger, Ernest Pascarella, and Amaury Nora, "First Generation College Students: Characteristics, Experiences and Cognitive Development," *Research in Higher Education 37*(1) (1996): 1–22.

8. Joan Ostrove, "Belonging and Wanting: Meanings of Social Class Background for Women's Constructions of Their College Experiences," *Journal of Social Issues 59*(4) (2003): 771–784.

9. Ancis, Sedlacek, and Mohr, "Student Perceptions." Dawn Johnson, Matthew Soldner, Jeannie Leonard, Patty Alvarez, Karen Inkelas, Heater Rowan-Kenyon, and Susan Longerbeam, "Examining Sense of Belonging Among First-Year Undergraduates From Different Racial/Ethnic Groups," *Journal of College Student Development 48*(5) (2007): 525–542. Williams and Ferrari, "Identification Among First-Generation Citizen Students."

10. Terrell Strayhorn, Meng-Ting Lo, Christopher Travers, and Derrick Tillman-Kelly, "Assessing the Relationship Between Well-Being, Sense of Belonging, and Confidence in the Transition to College for Black Male Collegians," *Spectrum: A Journal on Black Men 4*(1) (2015): 127–138.

11. Sandra Gonzales, Ethriam Cash Brammer, and Shlomo Sawilowsky, "Belonging in the Academy: Building a 'Casa Away From Casa' for Latino/a Undergraduate Students," *Journal of Hispanic Higher Education 14*(3) (2015): 223–239.

12. Ostrove, "Belonging and Wanting." Adrienne Swift and Margaret O'Dougherty Wright, "Does Social Support Buffer Stress for College Women: When and How?" *Journal of College Student Psychotherapy 14*(4) (2000): 23–42.

13. Philip Harris, "Who Am I? Concepts of Disability and Their Implications for People with Learning Difficulties," *Disability and Society 10*(3) (1995): 341–352.

14. Johnson et al., "Examining Sense of Belonging." Susan Rankin and Robert Reason, "Differing Perceptions: How Students of Color and White Students Perceive Campus Climate for Underrepresented Groups," *Journal of College Student Development 46*(1) (2005): 43–61. Williams and Ferrari, "Identification Among First-Generation Citizen Students."

15. Pauline Clance and Suzanne Imes, "The Impostor Phenomenon in High Achieving Women: Dynamics and Therapeutic Intervention," *Psychotherapy: Theory, Research, and Practice 15*(3) (1978): 241–247. Kevin Cokley, Germine Awad, Leann Smith, Stacey Jackson, Olufunke Awosogba, Ashley Hurst, Steven Stone, Lauren Blondeau, and Davia Roberts, "The Roles of Gender Stigma Consciousness, Impostor Phenomenon and Academic Self-Concept in the Academic Outcomes of Women and Men," *Sex Roles 73* (2015): 414–426.

16. Chammie Austin, Eddie Clark, Michael Ross, and Matthew Taylor, "Im-

postorim as a Mediator Between Survivor Guilt and Depression in a Sample of African American College Students," *College Student Journal 43* (2009): 1094–1109. Kevin Cokley, Shannon McClain, Alicia Enciso, and Mercedes Martinez, "An Examination of the Impact of Minority Status Stress and Impostor Feelings on the Mental Health of Diverse Ethnic Minority College Students," *Journal of Multicultural Counseling and Development 41* (2013): 82–95.

17. Cokley et al., "An Examination of the Impact."

18. Ibid.

19. Clance and Imes, "The Impostor Phenomenon."

20. Pauline Clance, Debbara Dingman, Susan Reviere, and Dianne Stobler, "Impostor Phenomenon in an Interpersonal/Social Context: Origins and Treatment," *Women & Therapy 16*(4) (1995): 79–96. Cokley et al., "The Roles of Gender Stigma." Mark Leary, Katharine Patton, Amy Orlando, and Wendy Wagoner Funk, "The Impostor Phenomenon: Self-Perceptions, Reflected Appraisals, and Interpersonal Strategies," *Journal of Personality 68*(4) (2000): 725–756.

21. Cokley et al., "The Roles of Gender Stigma." Leary et al., "Impostor Phenomenon."

22. Clance and Imes, "The Impostor Phenomenon." "Leary et al., "Impostor Phenomenon."

23. John Kolligian and Robert Sternberg, "Perceived Fraudulence in Young Adults: Is There an 'Impostor Syndrome'?" *Journal of Personality Assessment 54* (1991): 308–326.

24. John Kolligian, "Perceived Fraudulence as a Dimension of Perceived Competence," in *Competence Considered,* ed. Robert Sternberg and John Kolligian (New Haven, CT: Yale University Press, 1990): 261–285.

25. Michigan State University maintains a comprehensive listing of scholarships and fellowships for individuals searchable by population type: http://staff .lib.msu.edu/harris23/grants/3subject.htm, and Florida State University's Office of National Scholarships maintains a strong database of awards for underrepresented students searchable by identity category: http://onf.fsu.edu/node/61.

26. Juan Madera, Michelle Hebl, and Randi Martin, "Gender and Letters of Recommendation for Academia: Agentic and Communal Differences," *Journal of Applied Psychology 94*(6) (2009): 1591–1599. See http://www.csw.arizona.edu /sites/default/files/csw_2015–10–20_lorbias_pdf_0.pdf for an excellent guide to avoiding bias in recommendation and endorsement letters.

27. Thanks to NAFA colleague Jennifer Gerz-Escandón, who shared this strategy at the NAFA summer 2016 regional conference on diversity.

# 11

# "Thank Goodness for Gilman"

The Benjamin A. Gilman International Scholarship and the Balance of Resources for Merit- and Need-Based Scholarships

## BARBARA STEDMAN

*Barbara Stedman has been the director of National and International Scholarships as well as the Honors Fellow at Ball State University since 2007. Prior to those appointments, she taught in Ball State's Honors College and English Department, with a focus on Cultural Studies and environmental literature. She earned a PhD in English from Ball State in 1994, and in both her teaching and advising of students, she has drawn heavily on her international experience, especially living and teaching ESL in Pakistan and later establishing international classroom partnerships in Nepal, Egypt, and Venezuela. Outside of the university, she is very active in community organizations that serve the needs of Afghan women and children, support sustainable living initiatives, and protect the natural environment.*

In conversation last year, a fellow scholarship advisor shared that hers had been a year of finalists, alternates, and honorable mentions, but very few recipients—a fact that had been noticed by her superiors. "But thank goodness for Gilman! It saved my year!" she said. For her, it was one bright spot in an otherwise frustrating year of amazing applicants whose strengths and interests did not quite align with the goals of other scholarship competitions.

My colleague was referring to the number of successful Gilman International Scholarship Program candidates her university had celebrated over the past year, but her comment resonated with a different meaning for me. Gilman had likewise saved the year for a host of meritorious students with financial need. The program dispenses awards up to $5,000 to an enormous number of recipients each year—approximately 2,900 will be awarded this academic year—as opposed to the couple hundred or few dozen that other nationally competitive scholarship programs award.[1]

Open only to Pell Grant recipients planning to study abroad on short-term, semester, and academic-year programs, the Gilman Program targets a specific niche of students with financial need who may have no idea how they will pay for a study abroad experience. In the world of nationally competitive scholarships, such awards—which take both merit *and* need into account—are an important piece of the scholarship puzzle.

I was late in learning about the Gilman Scholarship. It was not until I attended a NAFA regional workshop in July 2010 that I heard about it. A wonderful day-and-a-half-long workshop at DePauw University included a session on the Gilman Scholarship. *Where had this program been hiding from me for a half-dozen years?* That fall semester, I found it tucked away somewhere in between my campus's study abroad office and financial aid office. Until that point, Ball State University had had only three recipients since the Gilman Program was launched in 2001, after being created by Congress the previous year.[2] No one on my campus had actively promoted the program or guided the few students who managed to find out about it and apply on their own.

Asked if I could "have" the Gilman Scholarship, our director of study abroad was only too happy to hand me oversight of the program. My first challenge was to get information out to potential applicants, and the only way to do that, I discovered, was to have my university's financial aid office send out an email to all Pell Grant recipients; I could not have access to the list of recipients myself. The emails went out, and I held an information session on the Gilman Scholarship at the beginning of the spring semester, with more than thirty students in attendance, rivaling only the number of students who came to Fulbright information sessions.

In my first application cycle, for summer 2011 study abroad, ten students applied for the Gilman Scholarship and two of them were awarded a scholarship. From fall 2011 to spring semester 2017, twenty-seven other Ball State students received the Gilman, in amounts ranging from $1,000 to $8,000 (thanks to a $3,000 Critical Need Language award added on top of a $5,000 scholarship). The students and I were all thrilled, and my university's administrators seemed pleased, but the nagging pressure from one of them lingered: *Sure, we are happy about scholarships like the Gilman, but where is our Rhodes or Marshall Scholar?*

I have done what all scholarship advisors do in educating high-level administrators about the value of the scholarship application *process* and the need to redirect their sole focus away from the tantalizing allure of national prestige. Still, a more practical question has remained: Can I justify dedicating a significant amount of my staff members' time and energy to a scholarship that is largely need-based, when our stated mission is to work with merit-based awards?

At Ball State, I am fortunate to have two staff members who assist scholarship applicants as the students draft and revise their essays. One of them, a current member of our English Department faculty, works with scholarship applicants for ten hours per week throughout the entire academic year. The other, a retired English instructor, advises scholarship applicants for ten hours per week during just the first half of each semester, when the workload is especially heavy due to Gilman, Fulbright, and other scholarships that have mid-semester deadlines.

While I personally dedicate a relatively small portion of my time each semester to the Gilman—mostly recruiting applicants, holding information sessions, meeting with individual students who have missed information sessions, and occasionally advising one or two students on their essays every semester—these staff members estimate that both devote one-third of their ten hours per week, during the first half of each semester, to Gilman applicants. In a small office like mine, that is a significant allocation of time and resources, especially considering that their work sometimes involves students who might not have a good chance of competing for a scholarship that is purely merit-based.[3] Can such an office justify the time spent, when there are so many other nationally prestigious scholarships that need promoting as well? For us at Ball State, the answer is absolutely *yes*.

Ball State is a mid-sized public research university in Muncie, Indiana. Of our approximately 15,000 full-time undergraduates, 36 percent are Pell Grant recipients, and many of those students simply would not have the opportunity to study abroad without the help of scholarships, like the Gilman, that consider both need and merit. While Ball State's scholarship advisors may dedicate more time to advising Fulbright applicants (for both the Fulbright U.S. Student Grant Program and the UK Fulbright Summer Institutes) and a range of other scholarship applicants, they find the Gilman among the most rewarding of their assignments each semester. One of them notes, "This is some of the most important work that I do. Gilman applicants will have fewer opportunities to study and travel abroad than some of our other scholarship applicants. I also think that they are often most in need of enriching experiences and most uniquely positioned to create change in attitudes toward cultural 'difference.'"

The other advisor also points out that "many [of our] Gilman applicants have never left the Midwest; others have traveled on mission trips to Central America, but very few have had the opportunity for cultural immersion" or even "dreamed they would have this opportunity while still undergraduates." Gilman applicants, in her experience, are among the most dedicated in drafting and revising their essays.

I wanted to find out if other universities similar to Ball State likewise value the Gilman Scholarship and put significant time and energy into recruiting and guiding applicants, so I looked at seventeen other universities considered by our Office of Institutional Effectiveness to be comparable institutions. These are all public, residential, research universities that offer similar academic programs and have similar student and faculty characteristics; seven are in the greater Midwest, and none are located in major cities. Their undergraduate populations range from approximately 9,500 to nearly 29,500, and, according to the College Navigator (part of the National Center for Education Statistics website), the average percentage of Pell Grant recipients in the 2014–2015 academic year among all eighteen schools (with Ball State included) was just under 28 percent; the median was 37 percent.[4]

Most of these universities, like Ball State, offer at least one Gilman recruitment session per semester. Some simply include the Gilman as one of several options when offering presentations on study abroad scholarships; others hold recruitment sessions dedicated exclusively to the Gilman. Most Gilman recruiters work with campus financial aid offices either to send out recruitment emails to Pell Grant recipients or to obtain lists of such students and send out the emails themselves.

For the majority of the institutions, the Gilman Scholarship Program is housed in the study abroad and international education office and is coordinated by a director, assistant director, or other staff member. Several of these study abroad offices also handle the Boren, Critical Language Scholarship, and Fulbright programs. One rationale for locating the Gilman Program in an international education office is that its staff members are intimately familiar with applicants' study abroad plans. These Gilman advisors may provide guidance and feedback to students as they draft and revise their essays, or they may routinely refer students to the campus writing center for help. At some institutions, such as Ball State, the Gilman is housed in an honors college or overseen by a faculty member or administrator dedicated to nationally competitive, merit-based scholarships. These Gilman advisors provide essay guidance and feedback from their own offices.

Regardless of where the Gilman Scholarship is housed, most of these advisors dedicate a significant amount of time, energy, and other resources to recruiting and advising applicants. Those institutions where advisors do not allocate much time to the program are also those where no more than a single Gilman scholarship was awarded during the two most recent academic years (2014–15 and 2015–16). For advisors who cannot dedicate much time and many resources to the Gilman application process, however, the Gilman Program provides information videos, webinars and other guidance on the program website that students may access directly.

Scholarship advisors who handle other nationally prestigious awards acknowledge the tug and pull of the Gilman Scholarship's relative importance. Do advisors value the Gilman? Definitely. Do high-level administrators on their campuses value the Gilman? Some value it highly; some do not.[5] As one director of nationally competitive scholarships put it, "Does my boss care about Gilman as much as Truman, Goldwater, or Fulbright? No." But that does not mean she cares any less: "I think it's a fabulous program that allows wonderful students to have experiences they would never be able to experience otherwise. It's a very fulfilling part of my work, for me personally."

Lindsay Calvert, director of the Gilman International Scholarship Program, also notes another way college administrators focused on "prestigious" national scholarships may see value in the Gilman Scholarship:

> We have data that substantiate that Gilman Scholars have a high selection rate when considered for other scholarships, especially the Fulbright Program. The Gilman focuses on undergraduates and setting them up for impactful experiences that then encourage and support their future application to post-undergraduate-focused national/international scholarships. For example, during the 2016–2017 selection for the Fulbright U.S. Student Program, more than 70 finalists and alternates were Gilman Scholars, with the majority awarded as finalists. These numbers have remained high for several years. In addition, in the first two cohorts of the Schwarzman Scholars Program, three Gilman Scholars have been selected through a highly competitive process and distinguished award.[6]

Beyond the value placed upon the Gilman Scholarship, I also wanted to see how one incredibly successful Gilman advising program balances its resources. I spoke with Michelle Ayazi, Study Abroad advisor at the University of California, Berkeley, which has one of the most successful Gilman advising programs, if not *the* most successful program, in the country. Although UC Berkeley is not among the seventeen "comparable institutions" that I was most interested in, I did want to see what Berkeley had done to produce 105 Gilman recipients in the 2014–2015 academic year and 95 recipients the following year. Ms. Ayazi generously shared tips that had proven successful for Berkeley—for example, publicizing the Gilman Scholarship widely on social media, unambiguously using a subject line of "Attention Pell Grant recipients!" in emails sent out to potential Gilman applicants, and, most important, involving past Gilman recipients extensively in recruitment of future applicants.

While all Gilman recipients are required to carry out a follow-on service project within six months of their return to the United States—a project that will "promote international education and the Gilman International Scholarship"—recipients from Berkeley have been wholly integrated into the recruitment and advising processes, thus reducing the time from Gilman administrators and advisors.[7] The program alumni not only give presentations on the Gilman Program and staff information tables at study abroad fairs; they even help review applicants' essays. Taking that kind of step in sharing responsibility and authority requires tremendous confidence and trust in one's students—and it has paid off in a big way for Berkeley's Gilman applicants. (The Gilman Program also supports requests for this kind of outreach on campuses and can identify program alumni to participate, even if one's institution may not have any available.)

Ultimately, for scholarship advisors at any institution of any size, the importance of the Gilman Scholarship—and any others like it that consider both merit and need—is grounded in the same value we place in all scholarships: the opportunities it makes possible for students in the short term and the doors that it opens for them in the long term. We have to continue educating others on our campus, doing the best we can with the resources we have, and thinking creatively about ways to balance them even more effectively.

## Notes

1. The Gilman International Scholarship Program is one of the U.S. Department of State's exchange programs for American students and is supported in its implementation by the Institute of International Education (IIE).

2. The program was created through the International Learning Opportunity Act and advocated by its namesake, former congressman Benjamin A. Gilman.

3. While most of Ball State's Gilman recipients have had GPAs of 3.5 or higher, we have had many in the 3.0–3.5 range, and a couple have had GPAs between 2.75 and 3.0.

4. The U.S. Department of Education's *Federal Pell Grant Program End-of-Year Report 2014–15* reports that the national average of Pell Grant recipients nationwide for that academic year was 36 percent.

5. Lindsay Calvert, director of the Gilman International Scholarship Program, via email correspondence with Barbara Stedman, February 7, 2017.

6. Ibid.

7. To learn more about Gilman's follow-on service project, see www .gilmanscholarship.org/alumni/follow-on-service-project.

# Part IV

## On the Profession

# 12

# Writing Self-Efficacy in Postsecondary Fellowship Applicants
## The Relationship between Two Types of Feedforward Treatments

**LAUREN TUCKLEY**

---

*Lauren Tuckley has served as the associate director of the Office of Fellowships, Awards, and Resources at Georgetown University since 2011. She earned a BA degree in psychology from Midwestern State University in her hometown of Wichita Falls, Texas. After her undergraduate training, Tuckley moved to London to pursue a certificate in existential psychotherapy from The New School of Psychotherapy and Counselling conferred by the University of Sheffield. She then earned an MA in social and public policy at Georgetown University, where her thesis centered on how social stratification impacts the national collegiate undergraduate attrition rate. Tuckley is currently a PhD student in Writing and Rhetoric at George Mason University where her research focuses on how writers' feedback orientation and self-regulation behaviors have an impact on the composing process. In 2016, she*

*was a recipient of a Fulbright International Education Administrators Award
to Korea. Tuckley was appointed as the NAFA communication director for
the 2015–2017 term.*

---

In the fall of 2016 a pilot study was designed to examine how the advising
process affects fellowship applicants' writing self-efficacy. The purpose
of the study was to contribute to the development of a set of scholarship
and fellowships advising practices, grounded in an extensive literature review, that allows for the testing of two different advising approaches to
determine if there are significant differences in these approaches as manifest in fellowship applicants' self-beliefs about their writing ability. While
this pilot study did not seek definitive prescriptions, it did seek to identify
potential pathways or frameworks for the rigorous testing and evaluation
of advising practices—to forge research pathways on *roads less traveled.*

## A Pilot Study: Writing Self-Efficacy and Applying for Competitive Fellowships

### CONTEXT & CONTRIBUTION:
### THE FIELD OF RHETORIC AND COMPOSITION

In 2003, Frank Pajares was one of the first to offer the field of rhetoric and composition a thorough literature review outlining the current
scholarly research on the relationship between self-efficacy beliefs and
achievement in writing.[1] This compilation served as the scaffolding upon
which the next decade's research on writing self-efficacy would build.
While this literature review drew from a wide variety of disciplines, from
educational psychology to composition theory, a common thread per-
sisted: a writer's belief in her writing ability is highly correlated with,
and often predictive of, a number of positive writing-related outcomes.
In the years that followed, writing self-efficacy served as a central theme
in scholarly investigations aimed at identifying individual differences in
writing ability and achievement—why some students of writing flour-
ish while others with similar writing instruction may struggle.[2] Writing
self-efficacy has received attention as collegiate writing centers and
champions of *writing across the curriculum* have sought to identify, de-

velop, and refine best practices for improving students' and scholars' written communication.

Fellowships advisors understand the significant role writing ability plays in the development of a well-reasoned, coherent, persuasive personal statement, but have less familiarity with how writing self-efficacy can have an impact on writing achievement in the context of fellowships advising. This study opens the discussion and identifies best practices in fellowship writing instruction as informed by writing self-efficacy. Grounded in social learning theory, this pilot study seeks to explore the relationship between writing self-efficacy and two types of "feedforward" writing instruction.

## Theoretical Grounding: Social Learning Theory

In the 1960s, Albert Bandura and Richard Walters popularized a fledgling sociocognitive learning paradigm aimed at more precisely understanding the principles that underpin and guide human learning behavior and development.[3] Their contribution in *Social Learning and Personality Development* advanced the social learning model, with its focus on self-referent beliefs. Ultimately, social learning theory supplanted the behaviorists' drive-reduction model for learning behaviors, which until that time was a favored model for interpreting the development of human agency and interaction.

Social learning theory posits that human agency, especially learned behaviors, predominantly relies on cognitive, vicarious, and self-regulatory processes. Learned behavior is more closely tied to the interior dialogue and beliefs that narrate one's agency—from goal setting to persistence in the face of challenges—than to environmental stimuli that inform but do not prescribe human behavior. What is termed *self-beliefs* are powerful motivators (and demotivators) of human agency. According to social learning theory, self-beliefs mediate the degrees of control one exerts in relation to given tasks. For example, if a student believes she cannot pass the exam, her self-belief informs the amount of energy and effort dedicated to activities related to preparing for the exam. The combination of cognitive perceptions, observations of others, and the degree of engagement in self-regulatory behaviors configures agency. With respect to the cognitive constructs that mediate agency, Bandura claimed that "how people behave can often be better predicted by the *beliefs* (italics added) they hold about their capabilities, what he called *self-efficacy* beliefs, than by what they are actually capable of accomplishing, for these self-perceptions help determine what individuals do with the knowledge and skills they have."[4]

Within the paradigm of social learning theory, the relationship among cognitive self-beliefs, vicarious observation, and self-regulatory behaviors is tridirectional, each node in the construct affecting the others and vice versa.

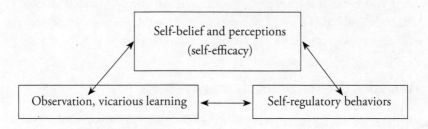

Since the popularization of social learning theory over fifty years ago, scholars have widely utilized the self-efficacy construct across a multiplicity of disciplines to theorize, frame, examine, and predict an astounding range of human learning behaviors: from self-beliefs related to academic achievement (e.g., I am going to ace/flunk this text), to perceptions related to athletic performance (e.g., I am picturing myself taking the shot off the tee), to the perceived likelihood of one's ability to lose weight (e.g., I cannot control myself around chocolate), to public speaking (e.g., I am going to choke or I love performing).

Examining the ways in which self-beliefs impact learning processes and goal-directed behavior is essential to furthering our understanding not only of the learning process in and of itself, but also, and perhaps more important, how to identify pedagogical strategies aimed at supporting the internal processes that mediate learning outcomes and achievement. Investigations that seek to uncover common internal processes related to learning behaviors will ultimately allow advisors to maximize each individual's capacity to develop and utilize new, or improved, skill sets.

Given the role that writing self-efficacy plays in mediating writing outcomes, it is natural to begin thinking about how fellowships advisors might further develop their advising processes and strategies with an understanding of how the writing process—particularly self-beliefs about one's writing capability—impacts writing performance and achievement. Understanding how the writing process functions is particularly important since it is the written piece that opens up the opportunity to advance a fellowship candidacy. The connection between writing success and writing self-beliefs laid the foundation for the development of this fellowships advising experiment; *would a fellowship applicant's writing self-beliefs be different if she were subject to one of two different "styles" of fellowships advising approaches?* This notion led directly to the design of the experiment.

## The Pilot: The Relationship between Writing Self-Efficacy and "Feedforward" Writing Interventions

This study sought to examine the relationship between fellowship applicants' writing self-efficacy and two distinct "feedforward" writing treatment interventions on two groups of postsecondary fellowship applicants.

## Context: Fellowships Advising and Feedback

In traditional postsecondary learning exchanges, there is often only one instance of feedback indicating the development or the mastery of a discrete skill or objective: the grade. Unless the student meets the assessor's learning expectations, a grade too often does not give the student the information that is needed to understand why expectations were not met or how to go about correcting an action so that the student can successfully meet the objective in successive attempts. Contrary to a single instance of feedback, when drafting written materials for a fellowship application, students have the opportunity to make multiple revisions, corrections, and adjustments in conversation with their advisors. Unlike traditional composition classes, the advisor is *not* the assessor of the final product; this allows the advisor to interact with the student in a coaching, rather than an assessing role.

Fellowships advising offers ample opportunities to engage with students through a variety of feedback processes and strategies. Given that fellowships advisors have a neutral, coaching-centered role in offering feedback to some "high-performing" students opting into the feedback process, examining how different types of feedback affect a student's writing self-efficacy may offer stronger predictive relationships. Fellowship candidates are likely to have a high degree of motivation and strong writing and academic self-regulatory behaviors. By studying this self-selecting population where these characteristics are shared, differences in treatment effects based on alternative models of feedback/feedforward interventions may control for other nontreatment effects (e.g., those related variances in motivation, self-regulation behaviors). In order to test how fellowship applicants' writing self-beliefs are affected by the differences in the way they are advised/coached, defining two distinct approaches to the advising process became imperative. The adapted framework used for this pilot study was derived from a popular model found in feedback treatment studies, namely the "Feedback Intervention Theory."

## FEEDBACK INTERVENTION THEORY

This study reinterprets the "Feedback Intervention Theory"[5] or FIT paradigm to distinguish between two types of writing interventions and their effects on fellowship candidates' writing self-efficacy.[6] Notably, the study departs from *feedback* as a source of intervention and rather offers writers *feedforward* instruction—essentially flipping the model and thinking of the feedback as a point of instruction. The *feedforward* approaches seek the same outcomes as feedback approaches: instruction aimed at achieving a goal or enabling mastery of a learning objective. Again though, *feedforward* is guidance or instruction that is offered *before* the writing begins or is assessed—and not afterward.

FIT posits that there are three distinct, yet interdependent, hierarchical processes occurring when an individual receives feedback. The recipient of the feedback focuses interpreting the feedback within one (or more) of these three categories: information related to the task (task learning), information related to the approach (task motivation), and information related to one's ability (self-efficacy). For example, a student receives the following feedback on his literature term paper: *"B–. Good effort, but some parts of the thesis or claim were unsupported by appropriate sources. You made an interesting argument, but several segments of the paper seemed rushed or incomplete. Outside of the troublesome claim issue, you're a good writer."*

There are many ways, depending on the student, that this information might be received and incorporated as feedback; but for illustrative purposes, the three different categories in the former example are shown in the table below.

| FIT Category | Feedback Information | Feedback Interpretation |
|---|---|---|
| Task Learning | Some claims were unsupported. | I need to work on adding reputable sources to support my thesis; that will improve my paper next time. |
| Task Motivation | Segments seemed rushed. | I should work on organizing my time more efficiently. I started writing my term paper way too late. |
| Self-Efficacy | You're a good writer. | Even though I made mistakes, I'm generally talented and can do better if I had more time. |

Clearly, feedback can be received and categorically interpreted as related to the task at hand (the objective or actions required to meet a goal), the method or strategy employed to execute the task (the various approaches taken to achieve a task or goal), and information related to one's inherent talent or ability to complete a task or achieve a goal. Consensus generally favors that the closer the feedback information is to the task-learning category, the more likely the recipient is to incorporate information that allows him or her to make the necessary improvements to move more closely to the goal behavior. For example, in the illustration above, receiving the feedback that "some claims were unsupported" is information that most helpfully allows the student to *change* his or her behavior to reach the intended/expected result in subsequent attempts. Again, according to FIT, feedback that is more closely grounded in task-learning information is more helpful in allowing the recipient to perform better or learn more quickly than feedback that provides the recipient with information about her task-performance strategy (motivation) or her inherent ability (self-efficacy).

The lion's share of information and advising that a fellowships advisor offers to an applicant comes well before the execution of the final goal behavior (i.e., submission of the final application or participating in a final interview). Given that a fellowships advisor's work comes *before* final execution, this study aimed at testing out the utility of a "flipped" FIT model (see the diagram below). *Would there be a difference in outcomes if students were offered "feedforward" instruction based discretely in one of the hierarchical categories?* While it can be assumed that instruction or feedback that addresses *each* of the categories would be most helpful, *what are the individual differences in instruction/feedback approaches?* These questions ultimately served as the treatment framework for this study and led to the development of the following research questions for this pilot study.

## Modified Feedback Intervention Theory: *Feedforward Intervention Theory*

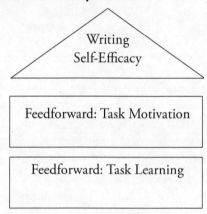

## The Research Questions

1. Based on the adapted FIT model, to what degree is writing self-efficacy temporarily affected by task-motivation feedforward (i.e., instruction)?

2. Based on the adapted FIT model, to what degree is writing self-efficacy temporarily affected by task-learning feedforward (i.e., instruction)?

3. To what degree are there differences in applicants' writing self-efficacy between the pre- and posttreatments for both the task-motivation and the task-learning treatment groups?

## The Sample

Postsecondary college students attending a selective, private, four-year university in the Mid-Atlantic were offered the opportunity to attend a writing workshop designed to help students prepare competitive applications for a scholarship designed to fund a language-learning, cultural immersion summer program. The first challenge that presented itself was sample size. In order to have a large enough "N" to divide the advisees into two separate treatment groups (i.e., task learning and task motivation) that would produce great enough variance to draw meaningful conclusions, the study was limited to a selection between two fellowships that were advised on at the study's university that would fit this population-constraining need. Since the study was piloted in the fall, the two options were then narrowed to one. This is how the study's prospective fellowship applicant pool was identified.

Each September, members of the student body are sent a mass email from the Office of the Provost to their university email accounts announcing the fellowship competition. The interest solicitation email was sent to currently enrolled freshmen through graduate-level students. The fellowship, a summer language program, seeks a diverse cohort—so freshmen through graduate students are encouraged to apply. Competition rates by degree level for this award are similar; there is no preference for graduate students compared to first-year applicants. Additionally, there is no disciplinary or academic preference that the fellowship seeks other than to secure a wide range of fellows across all disciplines, from STEM to the humanities to the arts.

The solicitation email announced the summer scholarship, explained what it is and what it seeks to achieve, when a student should apply, and offered dates for two upcoming writing workshops. These two different workshops would serve as the two treatment groups, but the students would not know there was a difference in instruction between the workshop offerings. In the solicitation email, students with an initial interest were encouraged to subscribe to the fellowship listserv in order to receive more information regarding the workshops and to be alerted when the registration for these two workshops opened up. From this initial solicitation, 215 prospective applicants subscribed to the listserv. The listserv was routinely emailed about the fellowship over the course of the next two weeks. The purpose of continued contact was to garner and sustain interest in the fellowship, so that a great number expressing initial interest would ultimately apply.

Approximately two weeks before the workshops were held, all listserv subscribers were emailed information announcing the workshop dates and offered links to the online reservation system where they could sign up for *one* of the two workshops. Prospective applicants were not allowed to register or attend both sessions because the workshop treatment groups were different, and it was this difference that served as the point of comparison for treatment effects. The maximum capacity for each workshop, held in the same location, was twenty-five registrants.

## Two Treatment Groups: Workshop A Task Motivation vs. Workshop B Task Learning

The registrations for both workshops were filled near maximum capacity. Workshop A was designed to offer feedforward descriptive instructions centered on *task-motivation guidance* (i.e., general strategies and best practices for how to approach writing without reference to the discrete question/essay). Workshop B was designed to offer feedforward strategies based on *task-learning conditions* (i.e., discrete advice on the best way to answer each question/essay). For more detail, see the table below.

| Workshop | Treatment Type | Session Content |
| --- | --- | --- |
| A | Task Motivation | • 15 min.: preliminary information (discussion of the fellowship, requirements, due date, etc.)<br>• 30 min.: "Effective Writing Strategies" (none of the direct essay questions were referred to)<br>  ○ Writing with the Audience in Mind<br>  ○ Narrative Writing: What Is It?<br>  ○ Cogency and Transitions<br>  ○ Asking for Help<br>• 10 min.: Postworkshop Survey |
| B | Task Learning | • 15 min.: preliminary information (discussion of the fellowship, requirements, due date, etc.)<br>• 30 min.: review of each essay question with examples of effective responses.<br>  ○ The entire application was reviewed question by question along with examples of previous effective responses. No higher-order writing strategies were offered.<br>• 10 min.: Postworkshop Survey |

*Note: Workshop attendees registered for the workshop date that best fit their schedules. Given that the workshops were offered on different weeks and on different days of the week, there may be limitations to the study's findings due to some unknown variance in attendee workshop selection based on availability preferences or restrictions.

## Self-Efficacy Survey: Pre- and Post-Assessments

Changes in applicants' writing self-efficacy were used as the measure to determine if there were treatment effects or variability based on assignment to treatment groups. Recall the importance of self-efficacy in performance of a goal behavior or task. Based on social learning theory, the higher degree of self-efficacy one has, the more likely one is to achieve a goal. Increases to applicants' writing self-efficacy may be correlated more positively with successful writing outcomes. The study aimed to measure movement in writing self-efficacy after having received a treatment (i.e., attending a writing workshop).

### HYPOTHESES

1. This study expects to find that *both* groups' writing self-efficacy ratings will increase from receiving either of the feedforward treatments.[7]
2. This study expects to find a greater degree of difference (an increase in writing self-efficacy) between the treatment groups, with the group receiving the task-learning treatment making the greatest gain in writing self-efficacy.

To measure writing self-efficacy of the fellowship applicants participating in this study, the Writing Self-Efficacy Scale developed by Albert Bandura and Barry Zimmerman was selected. This scale consisted of twenty-five items asking the respondents to rate their level of confidence on a scale of 0 to 100 for each of the items on the survey. The questions selected covered a range of issues pursuant to the writing process. Here are a few examples of the rated items:

- I can begin the writing process with no difficulty.
- I can adjust my writing style to meet the needs of the audience.
- I can come up with an opening paragraph to grab the reader's interest.
- I can write effective transitional sentences from one idea or paragraph to another.
- When I get stuck writing, I can find ways to overcome the problem.
- When I have a pressing deadline on an application with a large written component, I can manage my time efficiently.

The rating scale of 0 to 100 was used, as suggested by Bandura and Zimmerman, because it allows for the detection of change with greater degree of sensitivity. All participants were offered the opportunity to opt-in to the study by agreeing to take the pre- and post-assessments.

Those opting in were sent the Writing Self-Efficacy survey by email (taken through a Google form) one week before their assigned workshop. Afterward, at the conclusion of each respective workshop (and before the students departed the computer lab), they were again offered the same writing self-efficacy survey. The survey was de-identified, but required the participant to enter in a personalized code. The personalized code was used to match the pre- and post-surveys.

After each of the workshops had concluded and all the surveys had been completed and submitted, each group (the entire workshop cohort including nonparticipant listserv subscribers) received a video recording of each workshop (i.e., both the task-motivation and the task-learning sessions) to ensure that all applicants receive information from both sessions ahead of the final application deadline.

Pre- and postwriting self-efficacy surveys were administered. Raw data were analyzed to determine if there was a significant difference between the two treatment groups.

## Findings

### HYPOTHESIS 1: IMPROVEMENTS ACROSS BOTH GROUPS

|  | Group A: N = 24 (Motivation/Strategy) | Group B: N = 21 (Task Learning) |
|---|---|---|
| (Pretest) *Average* Writing Self-Efficacy Score | 73.87 | 76.19 |
| (Posttext) *Average* Writing Self-Efficacy Score | 72.52 | 79.53 |

### FINDING: INCONCLUSIVE

- Minor decrease in writing self-efficacy in the Task Motivation group, while there was marked improvement in writing self-efficacy in the Task Learning cohort.

## HYPOTHESIS 2:
## GREATER DEGREE OF IMPROVEMENT BETWEEN GROUPS

|  | Group A: N = 24 (Motivation/Strategy) | Group B: N = 21 (Task Oriented) |
|---|---|---|
| Pre- and Postdifference | −2.3 percent | 7.01 percent |

### FINDING: CONFIRMED

- There was a greater degree of improvement in writing self-efficacy for the group that received task-oriented feedforward instruction (task learning) compared to the group that received strategy-oriented feedforward instruction (task motivation).

## Further Research Prospects

### TOTAL IMPROVEMENT GAINED BY
### FIRST-GENERATION COLLEGE STUDENTS

In addition to survey items, several demographic questions were asked as a part of taking the assessment, from family income to grade level, to gender and race. One of the most interesting (non-hypothesis-related) findings was that, no matter which treatment first-generation college students received, their writing self-efficacy improved nearly 5 percentage points more compared to self-efficacy improvement gained by the traditional college students. It should be noted that this total first-generation "n" was 4 out of the 45 participants evaluated. While the total number of first-generation students in this study is too low to draw a definitive conclusion, it does indicate an area worth further exploration. That is to say, perhaps first-generation college students applying for fellowships experience greater gains in their writing self-efficacy through participating generally in writing-supportive workshops.

## Summary

The purpose of this study was to develop a set of scholarship/fellowships advising practices, grounded in an extensive literature review, that would allow for the testing of two different advising approaches to determine if there were significant differences in these approaches as manifest in fellow-ship applicants' self-beliefs about their writing ability. While this pilot study did not seek definitive prescriptions, it did seek to identify potential frame-works for future, rigorous testing and evaluation of advising practices—to forge research pathways in fellowships advising.

## The Future: Fellowships Advising and Research

More than twelve years underway, NAFA has grown from a score of fel-lowships advisors and foundation representatives in the late 1990s to an institutional membership count headed toward the 450 mark. We have moved from a fledgling band of advisors to a robust, thriving associa-tion. The progress to this point has been substantial, even remarkable, but there is also the growing recognition that it is time for our profes-sional association to "professionalize"—to take steps toward becoming an entity that not only offers support and guidance to its members, but one that contributes by setting standards informed by our code of ethics, establishes and promotes best practices, invests in meaningful opportuni-ties for professional development, and commits to the regular production of rigorous research on the work of scholarship and fellowships advising.

In keeping with the theme of this publication, *roads less traveled,* I call on members to rethink how we define and promote our craft. To go one step further: to identify advising practices and to test those practices by subjecting them to rigorous, literature-informed analysis. It is here, in the advising space between academic development and professional prepared-ness, that fellowships advisors support, coach, and nurture young minds. Fellowships advisors have the right to claim a foothold on the ladder of experiential, student-centered learning and the ever expanding horizons of cocurricular development. Every advisor knows this: that the fellow-ship process is first and foremost a transformational, learning-centered, cocurricular activity. Now, it is time to share our understanding with the higher education community at-large through meticulous and thoughtful research.

# Notes

1. Frank Pajares, "Self-Efficacy Beliefs, Motivation, and Achievement in Writing: A Review of the Literature," *Reading and Writing Quarterly: Overcoming Learning Difficulties 19*(2) (2003): 139–158.

2. M. Neely, "Epistemological and Writing Beliefs in a First-Year College Writing Course: Exploring Shifts across a Semester and Relationships with Argument Quality," *Journal of Writing Research 6*(2) (2014): 141–170; Eric Ekholm, Sharon Zumbrunn, and Sarah Conklin, "The Relation of College Student Self-Efficacy toward Writing and Writing Self-Regulation Aptitude: Writing Feedback Perceptions as a Mediating Variable," *Teaching in Higher Education 20*(2) (2015): 197–207.

3. Albert Bandura and Richard H. Walters, *Social Learning and Personality Development* (New York: Holt, Rinehart and Winston, 1963).

4. Albert Bandura, *Social Learning Theory* (Englewood Cliffs, N.J.: Prentice Hall, 1977).

5. Hendrien Duijnhouwer, Frans J. Prins, and Karel M. Stokking, "Feedback Providing Improvement Strategies and Reflection on Feedback Use: Effects on Students' Writing Motivation, Process, and Performance," *Learning and Instruction 22*(3) (2012): 171–184.

6. Avraham N. Kluger and Angelo DeNisi, "The Effects of Feedback Interventions on Performance: A Historical Review, a Meta Analysis, and a Preliminary Feedback Intervention Theory," *Psychological Bulletin 119*(2) (1996).

7. Note: It will be challenging to make any connective assumptions if both groups' writing self-efficacy improves to the same degree—so a significant difference within groups, but not between groups—that the effects can be attributed to either feedforward treatment and not to some sort of placebo effect.

# 13

# Reflections on the Value of Being in the Room Where It Happens

## ELIZABETH VARDAMAN

*Elizabeth Vardaman is an associate dean in the College of Arts and Sciences at Baylor University in Waco, Texas. An exchange professor in China and assistant director for several Baylor abroad programs in England and The Netherlands, she has traveled extensively on behalf of the university and led the first NAFA tour of British higher education. Her overview of that trip, "Keys to the United Kingdom," was published in* Beyond Winning: National Scholarship Competitions and the Student Experience. *She also authored "Coin of the Realm: Graduate Education in Britain," published in* Nationally Competitive Scholarships: Serving Students and the Public Good. *She has served as a scholarship advisor since 1998 and was a charter member of NAFA. She and Jane Morris (Villanova University) cochaired the 2006 NAFA Higher Education Symposia in the United Kingdom and the Republic of Ireland.*

## Part One: Then

Drawing on the Broadway musical *Hamilton* to establish my credentials for this musing, let me begin by saying, incredibly and without any merit, experience, or rap on offer, I found myself in 1999, 2000, and 2001 "in the rooms where it happens" over and over again. Those experiences gave me access to an important national conversation and established me as a credible purveyor of scholarship knowledge within my university. Revisiting that journey and reassessing those insights are pleasurable activities that, even now, remain somewhat instructive despite the intervening years.

I am proud to say I called the first of these meetings for Baylor, and the key person in the room with me for three days was Nancy Twiss, legendary and inspirational guru of all nationally competitive scholarships at Kansas State. As special assistant to the Provost for Scholarships at KSU, Nancy Twiss was involved with more than eighty students who became national winners, including a combined total of sixty Rhodes, Marshall, Truman, and Goldwater scholarships.[1] Having recently retired, she and her husband, Dr. Page Twiss, accepted my invitation to visit Baylor and gave us an eye-opening overview of the values and skills ideally embedded in a scholarship program. During a workshop she gave titled "What It Takes to Be a Winner," she advised us on first steps toward establishing an office and fused pragmatic nuts-and-bolts information with the nonnegotiable imperatives for students' self-actualization that should be foundational within academic institutions. She radiated a commitment to students and also embodied a gratitude for and a devotion to the genius of scholarship programs and the foundations that funded the scholarships: "Because of them, students all over the country are identifying issues central to their concerns, weighing what they want their lives to count for, and determining concrete steps toward achieving those ends."[2] She was a force and left an indelible impression on everyone with whom she interacted. Armed with reams of notes at the end of her three-day stay, I knew I would look back on her visit as a turning point in my career. I wanted to become a variation on the Nancy Twiss theme and, just as she had done, have a dramatic impact on the institution to which I was then and am now devoted.

Because Nancy alerted me to an upcoming conference that summer at the University of Arkansas, Fayetteville, sponsored by the Marshall Commission and Truman Foundation, I was there when the doors opened for "Breaking the Code." Codirected by Suzanne McCray, then director of the Office of Postgraduate Fellowships at Arkansas and Mary Tolar, then deputy executive secretary of the Truman Foundation, this ground-breaking conference introduced many academic leaders and advisors from a variety of higher education institutions to a world of scholarship competition fundamentals that had previously seemed, to me at least, almost hoarded away for use largely by a few renowned schools on the East and West coasts. The conference's overview of the Marshall and Truman scholarship schemes demystified the highly competitive awards to some extent and, more important for my own professional growth, introduced me to a cast of visionaries whose vast professional expertise has been vital for many years now to my own efforts at Baylor.

The seeds planted there germinated and flourished in various ways, generating a larger conversation among many academics on the importance of prestigious competitive scholarships to our own schools. Leaders from the Fayetteville gathering and others soon set in place another meeting. In the summer of 2000, a small number of individuals keen to look more deeply into these issues met at the University of Illinois in Chicago. And, yes, I was in the room. (I have never known how I received that golden ticket.) I recall gasping when someone suggested we launch a national organization to address the needs of scholarship competitions at universities nationwide. My response was quick and clear: "Oh, dear. Baylor paid my way to be here so I could help Baylor." What I meant by that everyone surely understood: I was intent on gathering insider secrets and using them strictly to help my own school. Dr. Jane Curlin, serving as a fellowships consultant at the time, responded with a gracious but also wry smile and then with compelling reasons why a national organization would indeed strengthen all of our individual efforts and have a formidable, positive impact collectively. She was articulate, experienced, and highly persuasive. That memorable meeting forged friendships and commitments that resulted over the next few months in the establishment of a charter and lift-off for the National Association of Fellowships Advisors (NAFA), with Dr. Bob Graalman, director of the Office of Scholar Development and Recognition at Oklahoma State University, as the first president of this fledgling enterprise.

NAFA, supported by many national and international scholarship foundations, held its initial conference in Tulsa, Oklahoma, in the summer of 2001. I recall being stunned to see that my name card one evening was set next to the place card of the director of the Truman Foundation, Mr. Louis Blair. We may or may not have had a conversation at our table that night not only because I had at that point only submitted one Truman application, but also because I was scheduled to give an address after the dinner and was quite nervous. When invited to be a presenter several months earlier, I should have responded with "Thank you, but no," since my scholarship experience was still largely theoretical. Instead I accepted for two reasons: All others from the charter group were extending themselves hugely to do their part for NAFA, and I knew without a doubt I would never be offered a leadership role again if I turned this one down. So I focused my research for the talk on the one topic I might conceivably know more about than others did—the values and accomplishments of the woman I most admired in scholarship realms. "Nancy Twiss 101: A Course in Transformation" gave me an opportunity to celebrate this remarkable standard bearer for our cause. People were generous about the presentation . . . but then it would be hard to give a boring talk on Nancy Twiss.

Having said "yes" to that opportunity also allowed me to be in a room where it felt like absolutely everything good was happening, including the unforgettable high note that concluded the conference. Dr. Gordon Johnson, director of the newly created Gates Cambridge scholarship scheme and chancellor of Wolfson College, Cambridge University, had flown in from England to affirm the formation of NAFA. In his keynote address the closing night, he introduced us to the Gates scholarship and proposed that the Gates Cambridge Trust become the first foundation sponsor for our newly formed organization. Such grand experiences do not happen to us often in life. A line from a James Wright poem "Blessing" best explains the feeling I am certain many of us had at that time: "Suddenly I realize that if I stepped out of my body I would break into blossom." But more important than the overflow of flowery feelings at that point, the challenging and rewarding work of building NAFA into a vibrant, complex, and essential organization was underway.

## Part II: Now

Fast forward fifteen years to the time when NAFA has become as essential as air to the busy enterprise of many scholarship offices across the United States. With over 400 member universities and scholarship foundations, it is robust with regional workshops, a vibrant listserv, study trips worldwide, biennial national conferences, and a national journal. Members are invested in NAFA committees, give cutting-edge presentations within NAFA and beyond on behalf of our organization, and invest deeply in serving our students well—a glance at our listserv verifies that. New voices of leadership emerge every year, asking important questions and addressing ever-evolving scholarship issues nationwide at the micro and macro levels. At home within our individual institutions, Jane Curlin was correct; NAFA members—whose expertise requires them to learn how to look at student development in a holistic way—may contribute significantly to a wide variety of efforts within the larger campus culture. They have the ability to remind other entities within the complex halls of higher education about some of the intrinsic purposes for which our schools stand, before and beyond garnering prestigious awards.

That is to say, today there are many other rooms where important decisions are being made and where NAFA advisors may be increasingly invited to the tables because they can bring privileged, valuable news and perspectives. Such meetings, enticing as they may be since they acknowledge what we have to offer, can be double-edged swords and quickly extend our responsibilities far beyond the terms of our contracts. Nevertheless, where scholarship advisors can find room to participate in think-tanks and task forces, the ripple effect for good to accrue to the campus culture can be sizable. The impact NAFA has had on the large enterprise of our colleges and universities is not yet documented in statistical reports, but some of the qualitative effects it has had on the functioning of our institutions shine out, no matter the outcome of win/lose tabulations at the end of the year.

Below I focus on anecdotes and stories drawn both from experiences at my own university and those shared by NAFA colleagues in order to illustrate at least some of the ways NAFA members are having an impact on the larger formal aspirational agendas at many schools. Of course, an advisor does not have to be a member of NAFA in order to have an impact on their campuses, but it is this constant sharing of best practices that helps give NAFA members a more confident voice, and that is the very purpose of this essay. Those who are not engaged in the ways described below may want to use such examples from their peers to create or broaden conversations on their own campuses.

- Engagement with NAFA has provided scholarship advisors a privileged place at some academic tables, such as Academies for Teaching and Learning (found under their various names in our institutions). There we advocate for increased ways students may access enlivened, active learning experiences, such as internships, service, and undergraduate research opportunities. Those needs can be substantiated in part on the proven value such engaged learning has had for distinguishing our young scholars and leaders as they bid for nationally prestigious awards. These activities, however, also stand on their intrinsic worth to individuals and to the joy of pursuing knowledge purposefully and linking it to their lives.

- Experienced advisors can speak authoritatively in many contexts about the importance of intense and creative efforts toward advisement across majors and departments—not just as a means to foster national awards. Enhanced advisement sets meaningful protocols in place and helps more students plan their futures, weighing options with the support of professional guidance. Advisor interaction with career center personnel seems essential and may foster students' gaining insights into talents and interests they have never before pondered.

- Conversations with personnel in academic programs (honors colleges, for example) and chairs of departments can open up new opportunities for undergraduates to understand the importance of and hone advanced skills in speaking, writing, and presentations.

- Sharing profiles of exceptional students with other campus committees has resulted in professors and departments being motivated to flip classrooms or place more emphasis on interaction instead of exclusively on lectures. One of my colleagues told a group about a Marshall finalist who had interviewed well in part because he had had responsibilities for teaching a class in his major field of study. Lights went off in several instructors' minds at that news, and dynamic new options were made available for some students the next term.

- When recruitment of high-achieving students is underway, advisors are the first to be called on for telling the stories of students who have maximized their education and made a significant impact on the campus culture or the wider community environs. Is there anything more mesmerizing at such a time than a narrative about a student who determined what was worth wanting and went after it hammer and tong? Additionally it should be noted that telling these stories in rooms where people who have "capacity" to fund programs are present can also yield new scholarship opportunities, all to the good for our students.

- NAFA members and their offices also develop partnerships across many entities with different perspectives and give diverse units a chance to interact with and savor shared values. Many NAFA advisors maintain a list of stakeholders who are committed to mentoring students and providing them the best advice possible for how to become engaged in service and leadership. The synergies at such meetings are positive and life-giving, even though they are not necessarily tied to the promise of great outcomes for students who make prestigious scholarship bids. The people who attend may not often be applauded for the work they are invested in but events like these emphasize that they deserve to be noticed and thanked for all that they do that is life-giving. Bringing these people together may galvanize resolve and renew people's energy across complex purposes and varied units, reminding everyone of their higher callings and the benefits of being a community.

- Some advisors have shared with their Registrar's office that its student transcripts are almost unreadable. Revised, electronic, bold presentations of those transcripts may be the happy result.

- Conversations with admissions personnel may enable them to understand more fully the importance of diversity and help them seek a more complex profile or set of characteristics within students' initiative and accomplishments in high school, qualities that extend beyond ACT or SAT scores. For NAFA members to serve on selection committees for creation and dispersal of in-house scholarship awards also provides insights and contributes to the design and implementation of such programs because trained advisors bring awareness of a complex set of issues that are invaluable to these deliberations.

- Volunteering to make a presentation to a Board of Governors or Regents on the impact of the scholarship office on the larger culture may not be a viable option, but being in *that* room to show the impact of a scholarship office on the larger campus culture can have long-reaching benefits.

The list could go on (I did not highlight, for example, the impact our work can have on study abroad or financial aid offices). The far-ranging applicability of our work explains in part why scholarship offices are housed in myriad places within a school. Thus the case might be made that our efforts relate to and enhance almost every other academic purpose.

Two final points remind us of scholarship advisors' potential contributions within our schools' broader goals: First, advisors see application recommendation letters that often take their breath away—usually in a positive manner. Faculty and staff invest hours in these efforts, but the resulting documents produced are rarely seen on campus by any other person beyond the scholarship office. Saying "thank you" to the writers may be the only affirmation they receive, yet their commitment to the students undergirds all the hope, aspirations, discipline, perspiration, and prayer that, like invisible silver wires, hold universities and students on task and moving forward.

Last, there is something ineffable, almost intuited, not unlike a felt presence on some campuses where the nationally competitive scholarship program interacts with many other academic entities. Sometimes the effect is charged with the electric voltage that has come from students who have prevailed in scholarship competitions. Hip, hip, hooray! Such achievements spark everyone's sense of what is possible, building a campus resolve to double-down and do better, do more, for all the students who have entrusted the college with their education.

But sometimes the felt presence of ideals, drive, energy, and resolve just moves like a spirit of inspiration among faculty and students, even when good fortune in the scholarship selection process did not come our way. As Nancy Twiss notes, "As the years passed, we saw that the University could help candidates, but we had not expected the reverse: that our nominees and the application process would affect the intellectual climate of the University."[3] It can and does where someone, perhaps a scholarship advisor or another administrator, has been in the rooms where amazing things happened and has instituted or revised important goals accordingly so that something valuable but hard to define winds itself throughout a community.

No Broadway musical by Lin-Manuel Miranda will result from the kinds of work we spend our lives doing on our campuses. But that is okay. After all, we are busy about issues that almost never culminate in dramatic duels at dawn (tempting as it has been once or twice to call someone out) or require fancy footwork and show tunes. Instead, our efforts are borne out one ordinary day at a time, often with no accompanying applause. Yet they continue to redound to the good for our remarkable students, our colleges, NAFA's mission, national foundations, and diverse partners and colleagues. And in the most important, solitary room of all (the one that goes with us everywhere, even into the still, small hours of the morning), advisors ponder, reassess, and sometimes reaffirm that their efforts make sense and that they matter. May we continue to nurture and protect that mysterious but important space and the necessary light and shadow cast there. For ultimately, it is the only place that can refuel us for the journey back into the complex, challenging, and often exhilarating fray of higher education.

## Notes

1. "Twisses Receive Lifetime Leadership Award," April 20, 2000, In View: Media Relations and Marketing website, http://www.mediarelations.ksu.edu /WEB/News/InView/42000twiss.html.

2. Nancy Twiss gave me a thirty-five-page manuscript containing excerpts from talks she had given during her career at KSU. I have quoted from that document here. In important ways that document has retained its vibrancy and seems as timely and wise today as it did in 1999. (Copies of this handout were available to people attending the first NAFA conference in Tulsa in 2001.)

3. Ibid.

# Appendix A

## SURVEY OF THE PROFESSION 2017

The NAFA Survey of the Profession is conducted biennially. The survey below was conducted in the spring of 2017 and resulted in 187 complete responses, which represents approximately 20 percent of the individual membership. Advisors may find the data useful in preparing strategic plans for their own offices, in seeking institutional resources, addressing staffing issues, and determining the right location for their offices. It may also provide insight into the work environments of some of their peers. As always, the results are a descriptive snapshot of the profession and are not intended to be used for other forms of analysis or for research purposes.

This survey was conducted by two members from the NAFA Communications Committee: Lauren Tuckely, chair, Georgetown University and Jennifer Gerz-Escandón, Georgia State University with support from Jesse Delaney, University of Arkansas.

### Gender
*Respondents indicated whether they were male or female.*

| | |
|---|---|
| Male | 22.0% |
| Female | 78.0% |

### Age
*Respondents indicated their current age range.*

| | |
|---|---|
| 26–30 | 8.6% |
| 31–40 | 31.2% |
| 41–50 | 31.7% |
| 51–60 | 21.5% |
| Over 60 | 7.0% |

## Race

*Respondents indicated whether they were American Indian or Alaskan Native, Asian or Pacific Islander, black or African American, Hispanic or Latino, white, or other.*

| | |
|---|---|
| American Indian or Alaskan Native | 1.1% |
| Asian or Pacific Islander | 1.6% |
| Black or African American | 4.9% |
| Hispanic or Latino | 2.7% |
| White | 89.7% |

## Salary

*Respondents indicated their annual salary range in their current positions.*

| | |
|---|---|
| Less than $50,000 | 16.9% |
| $50,000–59,999 | 20.8% |
| $60,000–69,999 | 23.0% |
| $70,000–79,999 | 16.3% |
| $80,000–99,999 | 14.6% |
| $100,000 or more | 8.4% |

## Education Level

*Respondents indicated the highest level of education that they have obtained.*

| | |
|---|---|
| Bachelor's or master's degree | 47.6% |
| Doctorate or terminal professional degree (MD, JD, etc.) | 52.4% |

## Title

*Respondents indicated their job titles.*

| | |
|---|---|
| Director | 39.6% |
| Assistant/Associate Director | 20.9% |
| Coordinator | 11.8% |
| Dean or Assistant/Associate Dean | 7.0% |
| Other | 20.9% |

## Faculty

*Respondents indicated whether they currently hold a faculty position.*

| | |
|---|---|
| Yes | 23.8% |
| No | 76.2% |

## Employment with Current Institution

*Respondents reported the number of years they have been employed at their current college or university.*

| | |
|---|---|
| 0–3 years | 26.6% |
| 4–6 years | 21.7% |
| 7–10 years | 16.3% |
| 11–15 years | 16.3% |
| More than 15 years | 19.0% |

## Employment in Current Position

*Respondents reported the number of years they have been employed in their current position as a fellowships advisor.*

| | |
|---|---|
| 0–3 years | 45.2% |
| 4–6 years | 27.4% |
| 7–10 years | 15.1% |
| More than 10 years | 12.4% |

## Fellowships Advising Experience

*Respondents reported the total number of years they have worked with fellowship activities.*

| | |
|---|---|
| 0–3 years | 27.0% |
| 4–6 years | 32.4% |
| 7–10 years | 18.9% |
| 11–15 years | 9.7% |
| More than 15 years | 11.9% |

## Fellowships Advising Appointment

*Respondents indicated whether their position is dedicated to full-time fellowships advising.*

| | |
|---|---|
| Full time | 43.0% |
| Part time | 57.0% |

## Fellowships Advising Appointment If Less Than Full Time

*Respondents with a part-time fellowships advising appointment indicated what percentage of their employment is attributed to work with fellowships advising.*

| | |
|---|---|
| Less than 20% of time | 15.5% |
| 20–39% of time | 31.1% |
| 40–59% of time | 24.3% |
| 60–79% of time | 21.4% |
| 80% of time or more | 7.8% |

## Daily Fellowship Workload

*Respondents indicated how many hours per day they spend on fellowship activities.*

| | |
|---|---|
| Less than 2 hours | 15.1% |
| 2–3 hours | 15.1% |
| 4–5 hours | 16.2% |
| 6–7 hours | 25.1% |
| 8–9 hours | 23.5% |
| 10 or more hours | 5.0% |

## Summer Hours

*Respondents indicated whether they have a nine-month base salary and, if so, how many hours per week during the summer they devote to fellowship-related duties.*

| | |
|---|---|
| 5 hours or less | 6.6% |
| 6–10 hours | 2.4% |
| 11–20 hours | 6.0% |
| 21 or more hours | 3.6% |
| I hold a 12-month appointment | 81.3% |

## Additional Duties

*Respondents indicated their job duties other than fellowships advising.*

| | |
|---|---|
| Teaching | 42.1% |
| Academic advising | 35.7% |
| Administering university-based merit awards | 35.7% |
| Honors programming | 30.0% |
| Undergraduate research | 30.0% |
| Career/pre-professional advising | 25.7% |
| Scholarly research | 20.7% |
| Study abroad/international | 17.9% |
| Service learning/community outreach | 12.1% |

## Career in Fellowships Advising

*Respondents indicated whether they plan to remain in fellowships advising as a career.*

| | |
|---|---|
| Yes | 45.8% |
| No | 14.8% |
| Not sure | 39.7% |

## Career Path

*Respondents indicated their intended career paths.*

| | |
|---|---|
| Fellowships advising | 47.0% |
| University administration outside fellowships | 33.3% |
| Faculty | 13.7% |
| Employment outside academia | 6.0% |

## Type of Institution—Public or Private

*Respondents indicated the nature of their institutions.*

| | |
|---|---|
| Public | 51.4% |
| Private | 48.6% |

## Type of Institution—Carnegie Classification

*Respondents indicated the nature of their institutions.*

| | |
|---|---:|
| Doctorate-granting universities | 57.5% |
| Master's colleges and universities | 16.8% |
| Baccalaureate colleges | 24.6% |
| Other | 1.1% |

## Size of College or University

*Respondents indicated the number of undergraduate students currently enrolled at their institutions.*

| | |
|---|---:|
| Fewer than 3,001 students | 22.9% |
| 3,001–9,000 students | 26.3% |
| 9,001–20,000 students | 21.8% |
| 20,001 or more students | 29.1% |

## Student Populations Served

*Respondents indicated all populations to which fellowships services are available.*

| | |
|---|---:|
| Undergraduates | 95.6% |
| Graduate Students | 62.2% |
| Professional Students | 35.0% |
| Alumni | 76.1% |
| Students at regional/satellite campuses | 13.9% |

## Nature of Office

*Respondents indicated if their institutions have an office dedicated to fellowships advising, or if fellowships advising is part of the activities of a larger office.*

| | |
|---|---:|
| Dedicated fellowships advising office | 42.5% |
| Fellowships advising activities are part of larger office | 47.5% |
| Other | 10.1% |

## History of Advising

*Respondents indicated for how many years dedicated fellowships advising has existed at their institutions.*

| | |
|---|---|
| 0–3 years | 21.9% |
| 4–6 years | 19.7% |
| 7–10 years | 20.8% |
| 11–15 years | 18.0% |
| More than 15 years | 19.7% |

## Location of Advising

*Respondents indicated where fellowships advising is organizationally housed at their institutions.*

| | |
|---|---|
| Office of the Provost/VP for Academic Affairs | 27.8% |
| Honors program | 26.7% |
| Office of the Dean/Associate Dean | 15.6% |
| Career/professional services | 7.8% |
| Other | 22.2% |

## Budget

*Respondents indicated the operating budget (excluding salaries) for their fellowships office or activities.*

| | |
|---|---|
| Less than $1,000 | 25.6% |
| $1,001–3,000 | 17.9% |
| $3,001–6,000 | 14.3% |
| $6,001–9,000 | 16.1% |
| $9,001–15,000 | 14.9% |
| More than $15,000 | 11.3% |

## Funding for Professional Development

*Respondents indicated whether they receive funds for professional development related to fellowships advising.*

| | |
|---|---|
| Yes | 89.2% |
| No | 10.8% |

## Funding for Student Travel

*Respondents indicated whether their institutions provide travel funds to students who have been invited for fellowship interviews.*

| | |
|---|---|
| Yes | 68.9% |
| No | 31.1% |

## Strategic Goals

*Respondents indicated whether they have strategic goals for their fellowships activities.*

| | |
|---|---|
| Yes | 59.8% |
| No | 19.6% |
| Not yet but plan to develop some | 20.7% |

## Means of Program Assessment

*Respondents indicated how they assess whether their fellowships programs are meeting goals.*

| | |
|---|---|
| No program assessment | 25.8% |
| Program self-review | 67.4% |
| Surveys | 32.6% |
| Benchmarking | 27.5% |
| Focus groups | 7.9% |
| Third-party evaluation | 2.8% |
| Other program-assessment tools | 5.1% |

## Data Collection

*Respondents indicated whether they collect data on various measures of participation and success.*

| | |
|---|---|
| No fellowship data collected | 7.3% |
| Number of students who receive awards | 91.6% |
| Number of finalists for various awards | 86.5% |
| Number of student applicants | 86.0% |
| Number of students meeting with fellowships advisors | 64.6% |
| Other direct measures of participation or success | 12.4% |

## Learning and Development Outcomes

*Respondents indicated whether they have created any learning and development outcomes for fellowship applicants.*

| | |
|---|---|
| Yes | 19.6% |
| No | 53.6% |
| Not yet but plan to create some | 26.8% |

## Learning and Development Assessment—Means

*Respondents indicated how they determine what students are learning from the application process.*

| | |
|---|---|
| No assessment of applicant learning | 54.8% |
| Student surveys | 31.6% |
| Essay reflections | 18.1% |
| Student focus groups | 5.6% |
| Third-party interviews | 2.3% |
| Other means of learning assessment | 10.7% |

## Leaning and Development Assessment—Schedule

*Respondents indicated when they evaluate what students are learning from the application process.*

| | |
|---|---|
| No assessment of applicant learning | 57.1% |
| Annually | 24.0% |
| After every fellowship application deadline | 14.3% |
| Each term | 3.4% |
| Other | 5.7% |

## Assessment Reporting

*Respondents indicated how they communicate assessment results.*

| | |
|---|---|
| No assessment results communicated | 37.7% |
| In meetings with university | 47.4% |
| In annual reports | 45.7% |
| On the office website | 8.6% |
| Through student interviews (in print, video, etc.) | 8.0% |
| Other | 4.0% |

## NAFA Resources

*Respondents indicated what NAFA resources they use most frequently.*

| | |
|---|---|
| Listserv | 96.3% |
| Conferences | 75.7% |
| Workshops | 40.4% |
| Website | 33.1% |
| Informal mentorship | 24.3% |
| Study tours | 20.6% |

## NAFA Website Resources

*Respondents indicated what NAFA website resources they use most frequently.*

| | |
|---|---|
| Resources Exchange | 41.7% |
| Contacts | 23.1% |
| Forums | 22.2% |
| File sharing | 7.4% |
| Other | 5.6% |

\* \* \*

## Supplemental Questions for Faculty Only
## Tenure

*Faculty respondents indicated whether they have tenure.*

| | |
|---|---|
| Yes | 38.6% |
| No | 61.4% |

## Faculty Assessment

*Faculty respondents indicated by whom they are assessed for the purpose of their annual reviews.*

| | |
|---|---|
| Administrative unit to which fellowships report | 52.3% |
| Home academic department | 13.6% |
| Both administrative unit and academic department | 34.1% |

## Salary Supplement

*Faculty respondents indicated whether they receive a supplement to their base salary for working with fellowships advising.*

| | |
|---|---|
| No supplement | 86.4% |
| 1–10% supplement | 4.5% |
| 11–20% supplement | 6.8% |
| 21–30% supplement | 2.3% |

## Salary Retention

*Faculty respondents indicated whether they would retain their base salary if they were not working with fellowships advising.*

| | |
|---|---|
| Yes | 72.5% |
| No | 27.5% |

## Release Time

*Faculty respondents indicated whether they receive released time from teaching for their fellowships duties.*

| | |
|---|---|
| No release time | 47.6% |
| 1–25% released | 26.2% |
| 26–50 % released | 7.1% |
| 51–75% released | 11.9% |
| 76–100% released | 7.1% |

# Appendix B

## THE NATIONAL ASSOCIATION OF FELLOWSHIPS ADVISORS EXECUTIVE BOARD AND FOUNDATION MEMBERS

### The National Association of Fellowships Advisors Executive Board

| | |
|---|---|
| Dana Kuchem, President | The Ohio State University |
| Kyle Mox, Vice President | Arizona State University |
| Jeff Wing, Treasurer | Virginia Commonwealth University |
| Brian Souders, Secretary | University of Maryland Baltimore County |
| | |
| Andrus Ashoo, Member | University of Virginia |
| Monique Bourque, Member | Willamette University |
| Robin Chang, Member | University of Washington |
| Robyn Curtis, Member | University of Southern Mississippi |
| Craig Filar, Member | Florida State University |
| Cindy Schaarschmidt, Member | University of Washington Tacoma |
| Jayashree Shivamoggi, Member | Rollins College |
| Stephanie Wallach, Member | Carnegie Mellon University |
| Sue Sharp, Foundation Representative | IIE/Boren |
| Lauren Tuckley, Communications Director | Georgetown University |

## FOUNDATION MEMBERS OF THE NATIONAL ASSOCIATION OF FELLOWSHIPS ADVISORS

ACIE-Critical Language Scholarship Program

American Association for the Advancement of Science

American Councils for International Education

American Friends of the Alexander von Humboldt Foundation

American Society For Engineering Education

Barry Goldwater Scholarship Foundation

Beinecke Scholarship Program

Cambridge Trust

Coro New York Leadership Center

Cultural Vistas—Alfa Fellowship Program

DAAD German Academic Exchange Service

Fannie & John Hertz Foundation

Gates Cambridge

Harry S. Truman Scholarship Foundation

Henry Luce Foundation

Honor Society of Phi Kappa Phi

Humanity in Action

Institute of International Education

Jack Kent Cooke Foundation

James Madison Memorial Fellowship Foundation

Knight-Hennessy Scholars Program

Marshall AID Commemoration Commission

Mitchell Scholarship Program

Morris K. Udall and Stewart L. Udall Foundation

Pat Tillman Foundation

Paul & Daisy Soros Foundation

Posse Foundation

Public Policy and International Affairs Program

Rangel International Affairs Program

Rhodes Trust

Robert Bosch Foundation Fellowship Program

Rotary Foundation of Rotary International

Steven A. Schwarzman Education Foundation

US-UK Fulbright Commission

Vaclav Havel Library Foundation

Washington Center (Pickering)

Watson Foundation

Winston Churchill Foundation of the U.S.

Woodrow Wilson National Fellowship Foundation

# INSTITUTIONAL MEMBERS

Adelphi University
Albion College
Allegheny College
Alma College
American University
Amherst College
Appalachian State University
Arizona State University
Arkansas State University
Auburn University
Augsburg College
Augustana College
Ball State University
Barnard College
Baruch College, CUNY
Bates College
Baylor University
Bellarmine University
Beloit College
Benedictine College
Bennington College
Binghamton University
Birmingham-Southern College
Boise State University
Borough of Manhattan
    Community College
Boston University
Bowdoin College
Bowling Green State University
Brandeis University
Bridgewater State University
Brigham Young University
Brooklyn College
Brown University
Bryant University
Bucknell University

Buena Vista University
Butler University
California Institute of Technology
California Polytechnic, Pomona
California Polytechnic State
    University
California State University, East
    Bay
California State University, Los
    Angeles
California State University,
    Monterey Bay
Canisius College
Carleton College
Carnegie Mellon University
Carthage College
Case Western Reserve University
Central College
Central Michigan University
Cerritos College
Chapman University
City College of New York—
    CCNY
Claremont McKenna College
Clark University
Clemson University
Cleveland State University
Coe College
Colby College
Colgate University
College of Charleston
College of New Jersey
College of the Holy Cross
College of St. Benedict/St. John's
    University
College of William & Mary

Colorado College
Colorado School of Mines
Colorado State University
Columbia University
Columbus State University
Concordia College
Connecticut College
Cornell College
Cornell University
CUNY Baccalaureate for Unique
    and Interdisciplinary Studies
Dartmouth College
Davidson College
Delta College
Denison University
DePauw University
Dickinson College
Doane University
Drexel University
Duke University
East Carolina University
Eastern Connecticut State
    University
Eastern Kentucky University
Eckerd College
Elizabethtown College
Elmhurst College
Elon University
Embry-Riddle Aeronautical
    University
Emmanuel College
Emory University
Emory & Henry College
Fairfield University
Fairleigh Dickinson University
Florida Gulf Coast University

Florida International University
Florida Southern College
Florida State University
Fordham University
Fort Hays State University
Franklin & Marshall College
Furman University
George Mason University
George Washington University
Georgetown University
Georgia College and State
    University
Georgia Institute of Technology
Georgia State University
Gettysburg College
Grand Valley State University
Grinnell College
Gustavus Adolphus College
Hamilton College
Hampden-Sydney College
Harding University
Harvard College, Harvard
    University
Hastings College
Haverford College
Hendrix College
High Point University
Hobart & William Smith Colleges
Hofstra University
Howard University
Hunter College
Illinois College
Illinois State University
Indiana University—Bloomington
Iowa State University
James Madison University

John Brown University
John Jay College of Criminal
    Justice
Johns Hopkins University
Juniata College
Kalamazoo College
Kansas State University
Kean University
Kennesaw State University
Kenyon College
Knox College
Kutztown University of
    Pennsylvania
Lafayette College
LaGuardia Community College,
    CUNY
Lake Forest College
Lamar University
Lawrence University
Lebanon Valley College
Lehigh University
Lehman College, CUNY
Le Moyne College
Lenoir-Rhyne University
Lewis & Clark College
Linfield College
Louisiana State University
Loyola Marymount University
Loyola University Chicago
Loyola University New Orleans
Lubbock Christian University
Luther College
Lynchburg College
Macalester College
Manhattan College
Marist College

Marshall University
Massachusetts College of Liberal
    Arts
Massachusetts Institute of
    Technology
McDaniel College
McKendree University
Mercer University
Miami University
Michigan State University
Michigan Technological University
Middle Tennessee State University
Middlebury College
Middlebury Institute of
    International Studies at
    Monterey
Minnesota State University,
    Mankato
Mississippi State University
Missouri University of Science and
    Technology
Montana State University
Montgomery College
Mount Holyoke College
Mount Mary University
Mount Saint Mary's University
Muhlenberg College
Murray State University
New College of Florida
New Jersey Institute of Technology
New Mexico State University
New York University
New York University Abu Dhabi
New York University Shanghai
North Carolina A&T State
    University

North Carolina State University
Northeastern University
Northern Arizona University
Northern Illinois University
Northwestern University
Oakland University
Oberlin College
Occidental College
Ohio Northern University
Ohio State University
Ohio University
Oklahoma State University
Olin College of Engineering
Oregon State University
Pace University
Pacific Lutheran University
Park University
Penn State Behrend
Penn State University
Pepperdine University
Pitzer College
Pomona College
Portland State University
Princeton University
Providence College
Purdue University
Queens College, CUNY
Queen's University Belfast
Quinnipiac University
Ramapo College of New Jersey
Reed College
Rensselaer Polytechnic Institute
Rhode Island School of Design
Rhodes College
Rice University
Roanoke College
Robert Morris University

Rochester Institute of Technology
Rollins College
Rosemont College
Rutgers, the State University of
    New Jersey
Salisbury University
San Diego State University
San Francisco State University
Santa Clara University
Schoolcraft College
Schreiner University
Seattle University
Seton Hall University
Siena College
Skidmore College
Smith College
Southern Utah University
Southwestern University
St. Catherine University
St. Edward's University
St. John's College, Annapolis
St. Louis University
St. Mary's College of Maryland
St. Olaf College
St. Peter's University
Stanford University
Stonehill College
Stony Brook University
SUNY at Buffalo
SUNY Cortland
SUNY Geneseo
SUNY New Paltz
SUNY Old Westbury
SUNY Oswego
Susquehanna University
Swarthmore College
Syracuse University

Temple University
Tennessee Technological University
Texas A&M University
Texas A&M University-Kingsville
Texas State University
Texas Tech University
The Citadel
Trinity College
Trinity Valley Community College
Truman State University
Tufts University
Tulane University
Union College
Union University
United States Air Force Academy
United States Coast Guard
    Academy
United States Military Academy
University at Albany
University College London
University of Alabama
University of Alabama at
    Birmingham
University of Alaska Anchorage
University of Arizona
University of Arkansas
University of Arkansas at Pine
    Bluff
University of Arkansas Clinton
    School of Public Service
University of California, Berkeley
University of California, Davis
University of California, Irvine
University of California, Los
    Angeles
University of California, Riverside
University of California, San Diego

University of California, Santa
    Barbara
University of Central Arkansas
University of Central Florida
University of Chicago
University of Cincinnati
University of Colorado at Boulder
University of Connecticut
University of Dallas
University of Dayton
University of Delaware
University of Denver
University of Florida
University of Georgia
University of Hawaii at Manoa
University of Houston
University of Idaho
University of Illinois at
    Chicago
University of Illinois at Springfield
University of Illinois at Urbana-
    Champaign
University of Iowa
University of Kansas
University of Kansas Medical
    Center
University of Kentucky
University of London
University of Louisville
University of Maryland, Baltimore
    County
University of Maryland, College
    Park
University of Massachusetts
    Amherst
University of Massachusetts Lowell
University of Memphis

University of Miami
University of Michigan, Ann Arbor
University of Minnesota
University of Minnesota, Morris
University of Mississippi
University of Missouri—Columbia
University of Missouri—Kansas
  City
University of Montana
University of Nebraska at Kearney
University of Nebraska—Lincoln
University of Nebraska at Omaha
University of Nevada at Las Vegas
University of Nevada at Reno
University of New Hampshire
University of New Mexico
University of North Alabama
University of North Carolina at
  Chapel Hill
University of North Carolina at
  Charlotte
University of North Carolina at
  Greensboro
University of North Carolina at
  Wilmington
University of North Dakota
University of North Florida
University of North Georgia
University of North Texas
University of Northern Iowa
University of Notre Dame
University of Oklahoma
University of Oregon
University of Pennsylvania
University of Pittsburgh
University of Portland
University of Puget Sound

University of Rhode Island
University of Richmond
University of Rochester
University of San Diego
University of Scranton
University of South Alabama
University of South Carolina
University of South Dakota
University of South Florida
University of Southern California
University of Southern Mississippi
University of Tennessee
University of Tennessee at
  Chattanooga
University of Texas at Dallas
University of Texas Rio Grande
  Valley
University of the Pacific
University of Toledo
University of Tulsa
University of Vermont
University of Virginia
University of Washington
University of Wisconsin—
  Madison
University of Wisconsin—Eau
  Claire
Ursinus College
Utah State University
Utah Valley University
Valparaiso University
Vanderbilt University
Vassar College
Villanova University
Virginia Commonwealth
  University
Virginia Military Institute

Virginia Tech University
Wabash College
Wake Forest University
Washington and Lee University
Washington College
Washington State University
Washington University in St. Louis
Wellesley College
Wesleyan University
Western Carolina University
Western Kentucky University
West Virginia University
Western Washington
   University
Westminster College

Westmont College
Wheaton College (MA)
Whitman College
Whittier College
Wichita State University
Willamette University
Williams College
Winthrop University
Worcester Polytechnic Institute
   (WPI)
Yale University
Yale-NUS College
Yeshiva University
Young Harris College

# Index

194 • *Index*

Practice for All Experiential Learning Activities, 59–60
National Survey of Student Engagement, 61
need-based aid, 1
networks, ix, 115
New York University, 4
NOAA (National Oceanic and Atmospheric Administration) Hollings scholarships, 72
nomination letters. *See* letters of endorsement
nontraditional students, recruitment of, 114. *See also* underrepresented students
North Carolina A&T, multicultural recruitment of, 115

Oakland, 2015 NAFA conference in, vii, 1
Obama, Barack, 33
Ohio State University, The, ix, 183, 188
100 Percent Engagement Initiative (University of Arizona), 56–57
online applications, 28, 41
outreach, to underrepresented students, 128–129
overpreparation, for Truman Scholarship interviews, 41–49

Pajares, Frank, 146
Parish, Carol, 29
Partnership for Public Service, 70
partnerships on campus, 3, 4. *See also* collaboration
Peace Corps, 72, 91
Pell grants, 73, 115, 138, 141n4; Gilman Scholarship and, 136, 139
Perimeter College, 5
Pew surveys, on millennials, 13
PhD degree, 70–71
Philadelphia, 2017 NAFA conference in, viii
Pickering Foundation, vii, 73, 184
Portnoy, Jeff, 114
postgraduate scholarship competitions, 23–24
Presidential Management Fellowship (PMF) Program, 4, 66, 70–71
Princeton scholarships, 71
privilege, tradition of, 122
professional development, 4, 158, 177
Public Policy and International Affairs Program, vii, 184
public service, 2, 12, 17, 54, 67, 70; Truman Scholarships and, 45, 71. *See also* government service

Rangel grants, 73
Read, Amanda, 38
recruitment, 1, 27, 67, 71; for Madison scholarships, 3, 37; of underrepresented fellowship candidates, vii, 112–119, 128–129
reflection, by students, 59–60, 62, 88
registrar's office, 167
Rhodes Scholarships, 23, 24, 71, 86, 94
Rich, Andrew, 11, 17n1, 42; "Public Service, Power, and the Challenges Facing Millennials," 2, 11–17
Richardson, John, viii, 11, 12
Rivers, Lee, 116–117
"The Road Less Traveled" (8th NAFA biennial conference), vii, 1, 2
Roosevelt Institute, 11
Rotary scholarship, vii
Royal Society of Arts, 92

Salisbury State University, 5
Sangupta, Sagaree, 37
Šaras, Emily Daina, 132n1
scholarship advising and advisors, 66, 68–69, 71, 168; campus culture impacted by, 165–169; student engagement and, 55, 61–62. *See also* fellowship advisors; fellowships advising
scholarship process and scholarships, ix, 70, 122, 125, 126; campus, 113, 167
Schug, David, 4, 92; "Bela Karolyi's Handstand: The Whys and Hows of Letters of Endorsement," 91–106
Schwarzman Scholarship, 1, 94, 140, 184
science, 20, 21–23. *See also* STEM disciplines
security clearance, 4, 66, 73–74
self-beliefs, 147, 148, 149
self-efficacy, 148
service, 140; to students, 2, 3, 131. *See also* government service; public service
service learning, 56, 58. *See also* student engagement
Silicon Valley, 15
Simula, Brandy, 121, 132n1; "Belonging, Impostor Phenomenon, and Advising Students from Underrepresented Backgrounds," 5, 121–134
social entrepreneurship, 2, 14
social learning theory, 147–148, 155
social media, 47, 140. *See also* Facebook; LinkedIn